# LOOKING BACK

## A Tail Gunner's View of WWII

### By

### Dale VanBlair

This book is a work of non-fiction. Names and places have been changed to protect the privacy of all individuals. The events and situations are true.

ISBN: 1-4140-0817-1 (e-book)
ISBN: 1-4140-0816-3 (Paperback)
ISBN: 1-4140-0815-5 (Dust Jacket)

Library of Congress Control Number: 2003097251

This book is printed on acid free paper.

Printed in the United States of America
Bloomington, IN

1stBooks - rev. 10/23/03

Dedicated to the memory of my wife of fifty-three years,

Mary Elizabeth, whom I lost to cancer in September, 2002.

She had a special gift for loving people.

*The bustle in a house*

*The morning after death*

*Is solemnest of industries*

*Enacted upon earth,—*

*The sweeping up the heart*

*And putting love away*

*We shall not want to use again*

*Until eternity.*

—Emily Dickinson

# CONTENTS

# PREFACE

He that outlives this day, and comes safe home,

Will stand a tip-toe when the day is named,

And rouse him at the name of Crispian...

Old men forget; yet all shall be forgot,

But he'll remember with advantages

What feats he did that day; then shall our names,

Familiar in his mouth as household words...

Be in their flowing cups freshly remember'd.

This story shall the good man teach his son;

And Crispin Crispian shall ne'er go by,

From this day to the ending of the world,

But we in it shall be remember'd;

*We few, we happy few, we band of brothers;*

*For he today that sheds his blood with me*

*Shall be my brother...*[italics added]

William Shakespeare, *Henry V, act iv*

This is the story of my own Band of Brothers, the Alfred H. Locke B-24 crew, stationed first at Seething, then at Hethel, England, after training with the 448th Bomb Group at Wendover Field and Sioux City Army Air Base.  It is to their memory and to honor our part in World War II that I dedicate this tale.

But especially, this is for Albert (Shorty) Spadafora, my friend who was more than a friend, whose death left a void in my life that no one else could fill.  The bond we shared taught me that you can be brothers though born of different mothers and that time does not lessen the loss nor dim the memories.

Credit for initiating this project must go to my older daughter, Debbi, who in 1989 insisted that I write an account of my time in the United States Army Air Forces during WWII.  After resisting her repeated requests (sometimes called nagging) for several months, I finally reluctantly began writing.  Because forty-four years had at that time elapsed since my discharge, I was certain that recalling events worth writing about and coming up with details of those that I did recall would be a major challenge.  However, I found that the scrapbook which I compiled soon after my discharge was invaluable in jogging my memory and in providing exact dates, for it contained such items as newspaper clippings about missions which I had made, special orders involving transfers and promotions, weekend passes to London, receipts for London hotel rooms, and a miscellany of other memorabilia (I was a packrat then and, much to my wife's disapproval at times, still am). I also had the 1944 diary in which I had made brief entries about each of my missions and a few other events. A packet of my letters, most of which I had written while overseas, that Mother had kept was of some help, as were a few essays which had survived from a college creative writing course taken in 1946 in which I made use of service experiences. *The 1000 Day Battle*, by James Hoseason, a history of the 448th Heavy Bombardment Group provided an excellent supplement to my memory. Also, I found that as I wrote, my memory retrieved incidents and details from my service days that had been long buried.

After completing the first account in 1989, other things came to mind that needed to be added. The result was a revision a year later that added several pages, and I thought I was finished. I was mistaken. Subsequently, more details cropped up in my memory, followed by a reunion with John Hortenstine, our crew's navigator, in 1992 that provided additional information. After acquiring a computer in 1994, I put my WW II memoirs on a disk so that I could at any time enter anything new that came to mind.

In August, 2000, my pilot's granddaughter, Melinda Staley, and I found each other through the internet. Melinda supplied valuable information from her grandfather's letters and other memorabilia concerning such things as dates, planes we flew, and the last mission our crew made. She also made contacts via the internet that resulted in useful material. Also, I must thank Mike Bailey, who very kindly gave me permission to copy photos from his book *Liberator Album: B-24s of the 2nd Air Division, USAAF*.

I originally wrote down my experiences solely for my immediate family and had no thought whatsoever about publication. As friends and acquaintances found out about my narrative, they asked to read it, and contacts made via the internet resulted in its being read by others. Many of those who read it gave me positive feedback, and several of them suggested that I look into having it published. That feedback and the continual encouragement to seek a publisher that I received from Debbi and Melinda finally convinced me to carry through.

Dale VanBlair

# CHAPTER 1: THE EARLY YEARS

Born June 17, 1921, in Quincy, Illinois, I was for fourteen years the only child in a family that included, besides my parents, doting grandparents and Mother's two sisters and two brothers and their spouses (the first of my three cousins did not arrive on the scene until 1935). When I was five, Mother and Dad, Grandma and Granddad Orr and Mother's siblings, who were still unmarried, moved into an eight-room house. We lived in the upstairs apartment, Mother's brother Charlie slept in another upstairs room, and the others all lived downstairs. Even though it was a large house, as I look back I wonder how eight people managed as well as we seemed to, especially with only one bath. What made it possible, I'm sure, is that the Orrs were a close-knit family who enjoyed being together, and Dad fit into the family quite well.

The situation was perfect for me to turn into a spoiled brat, but neither Dad nor Mother put up with any nonsense. Dad was especially strict and quick to turn me over his knee or apply a switch to my legs. While Mother did not spank me very often, she didn't hesitate if she felt it was necessary. On one occasion she washed my mouth out with soap because I got a little sassy. I knew I was loved, but I also knew I had better obey.

I was almost nine years old before marriages began to reduce the population in our house. Between June, 1929, and December, 1930, two of my aunts and one uncle got married, moved out and were no longer available to give me attention on a daily basis. I survived, but just barely.

I visited my Grandma VanBlair (her husband had died when my dad was quite young) and her sister, Belle, frequently. They also lived in Quincy and ran a boarding house in an old, brick, two-story duplex, one half of which was occupied by other renters. Grandma and Aunt Belle rented two upstairs bedrooms to men and provided meals for them and a few other men, the latter of whom ate only their evening meals there. Until the owner of the duplex wired it for electricity in the late 1920s, kerosene lamps provided light. Grandma and Aunt Belle sometimes baby-sat me (no hired baby sitters for me!) during evenings when Mother and Dad were going out; and while I liked Grandma very much (Aunt Belle was all right but could sometimes be a little grouchy), I was always glad when my parents came to pick me up, for I found the lamp-lit house to be a little gloomy and forbidding. I enjoyed visiting them during the day, however, for they lived close to the downtown business section and would frequently take me to one of the stores that sold toys, let me look around, and sometimes buy me something.

Besides not having the best of personalities, Belle sometimes made my parents angry by inferring they were not making the best decisions where I was concerned. When I was in the fourth grade, Mother and Dad, much to my delight, decided that I should no longer have to wear long underwear during the winter. Belle thought that was terrible and made a trip to my school to talk to Miss Shanahan, the principal, about the matter. I don't know what my principal told Belle, but she called Mother, whom she knew, to tell her about Belle's visit, which she found quite humorous. Mother did not think it was funny and was furious. I never knew if she confronted Belle about the visit but doubt if she did, for she preferred to avoid controversy.

The basis for my present love of fishing goes back to my early childhood. The whole Orr clan liked to fish and frequently got

3

together for fishing trips to some local stream or lake. I can still remember the thrill of catching my first fish, a bluegill that was probably too small to keep but which went on the stringer because I had caught it. I also remember the time when Aunt Elsie, who was fishing beside me, caught a nice fish and got so excited that she jumped up and down and stepped on my straw hat, which I had laid on the ground nearby. I yelled at her to get off my hat, which made her laugh, which in turn made me still more indignant. I was reminded of that incident occasionally at family get-togethers even into my early adult years.

Christmas was a magical time for me, especially during the years that my aunts and uncles were still single and living downstairs. After Thanksgiving was behind, they would begin asking me, "What do you think old Santa Claus will bring you?" or "What do you want Santa to bring you?" I had plenty of answers, of course, and they no doubt made mental notes of what they might buy. I dutifully dictated my letter to Santa to Mother and watched as she placed it in an envelope and addressed it. On Christmas Eve, our church always put on a program, which included Santa appearing to pass out presents that had

4

been placed under the big Christmas tree, which was always a cedar tree that someone had cut and brought in. My parents, of course, always saw that there was something for me. The program consisted primarily of children reciting poems or singing Christmas songs. I was always given a Christmas poem to memorize and recite, which I didn't like to do but which my parents strongly hinted was expected of me. On Christmas morning there was the excitement of nine people opening gifts and expressing their pleasure at what they had received. After Mother's two sisters and younger brother married, their spouses added three more to our group. Mother and Dad and I always had our own little Christmas upstairs before going down to join the rest of the family.

All the Orrs except Granddad attended Madison Park Christian Church faithfully and served in various capacities. Why he stayed home while everyone else went to church Sunday morning and evening, I don't know. When the members decided to build a new sanctuary and do much of the work themselves, he spent many hours helping but did not attend services. When he was in his seventies, he finally was baptized and joined the church.

Dad grew up in the Methodist church, but after he and Mother were married, he began attending Madison Park, although he sometimes skipped a Sunday. After World War II he was baptized, joined the church, and ultimately served as a deacon. Mother, of course, took me every Sunday, and at age twelve I accepted Christ as my Savior and was baptized, even though Aunt Belle thought I was too young. I participated in the youth activities, and when the church began sponsoring a scout troop when I was fourteen, I joined it. During the next four years I progressed through Life Scout and was close to qualifying for Eagle Scout when I dropped out on graduating from high school.

My parents and the rest of the family thought that I was quite intelligent and would do well in school. My first report card, however, was a disaster, and my parents were dismayed. A majority of my grades were F's. Mother immediately had a conference with Miss Duncan, my first-grade teacher, and discovered that I had somehow been given the wrong books. Once I had the right ones, I proved that I wasn't a dummy after all. The fiasco proved to be a financial windfall for me, however. At the beginning of the second grading period, Mother's youngest sister, Alma, promised me a dime

for every A that I made, and it cost her dearly the rest of the semester,

for I made mostly A's. At the beginning of the second semester, she

cut back to a nickel for each A. Throughout grade school, I was at or

near the top of the honor roll when it was posted each grading period.

I did not do quite as well in high school but was in the upper ten

percent of my graduating class. My parents expected me to use the

ability I had, and I knew I had better do so if I wanted to avoid being

reprimanded for slacking off.

The Great Depression that followed the stock market crash in

1929 took about three years to have a major impact on Dad's job as a

machinist at Gardner-Denver Company, one of the major industries in

Quincy. In fact, in 1930 my parents signed a contract to buy their

first house and moved out of the apartment above my grandparents.

Within two years, however, Dad's work was cut back so much that

they could no longer afford the house payments, and we moved back

into the apartment we had left two years earlier. Because Dad was

being called to work at Gardner-Denver so infrequently, he signed up

for WPA (Works Progress Administration) to make ends meet. Jokes were frequently told about how the men on WPA jobs were seen leaning on their shovels or otherwise loafing, but Dad would not have been one of them. His work ethic was too strong to let him not give a fair return for his pay. Because she probably could not have rented the house if we were forced to move, Mrs. Baker, our landlord who lived nearby, let us stay without paying rent until the time came when we could afford to do so. I suspect she figured it was better to have someone living in the house and taking care of it than to let it sit empty.

We qualified for certain free food items, one of which was flour, so Mother began baking bread for the first time in her life. The first loaves weren't all that great, but she soon began turning out excellent bread. I loved the smell of the freshly baked bread and frequently got a slice of warm bread.

To save the cost of coal, Dad and Granddad got permission from a landowner to cut down dead trees, which they cut up to burn in the heating stoves. Some of the wood was usually stacked behind the downstairs kitchen stove, and I spent many hours building houses and other things with the smaller pieces.

As a child, I didn't give much thought to the fact that we were poor. In fact, the depression did not have a great impact on my life. There was always ample food on the table, my clothes weren't patched, and I always received presents on my birthday and at Christmas. Although they never said so, Mother and Dad undoubtedly went without so that they would have money to provide things that I did not necessarily need but wanted.

The hard times actually benefited me in two ways: I once again was living in the same house with my grandparents, and my parents could not afford to keep paying for the piano lessons that I disliked, primarily because I hated to practice.

It was probably in the spring or summer of 1933 that Dad's work picked up enough that we could afford to rent a house directly across the street from my grandparents. I doubt if Dad and Mother paid more than $10 a month, quite possible less, for landlords were happy to get whatever they could out of rental property. It was an old two-story brick house which was bigger than we needed, but I suspect my parents rented it because the price was right.

By early 1937, when I was a sophomore in high school, Dad and Mother had saved enough to make a down payment on another house which they purchased for $1500. Although it dated to probably the 1890s or early 1900s, it was in good condition and met our needs quite well. For the first time, we even had a coal furnace that kept the entire house comfortably warm. Dad also felt financially secure enough to trade in our very old car on a 1934 Chevrolet, which I learned to drive when I was a junior.

During my senior year my parents and I discussed the possibility of my going to college. If I were to go, it would be necessary for me to work to pay part of the cost. A representative from Western Illinois University at Macomb, Illinois, came to the house to explain such things as the cost, my chances of getting a part-time job, and the curriculum. Even though I had done well in school, I had never particularly liked going to school and was not too enthusiastic about enrolling in college. I preferred finding a job. In view of my attitude and the fact that college would impose a financial burden on them, we agreed that after graduating from high school, I would go to work and, if I so desired, consider college the following year.

# CHAPTER 2: MAKING THE DECISION

When I graduated from high school in 1939, the economy was still not fully recovered from the Great Depression, and jobs were not easy to find in my home town of Quincy, Illinois. I filed applications at several businesses, but nothing opened up for me during the summer. Then, about the middle of September, Dad came home one afternoon with the news that he could get me a job as an apprentice machinist at the factory, Gardner-Denver Company, where he had worked as a machinist for about twenty years. As a result of increased defense spending, Gardner-Denver was receiving government contracts to produce pumps and air compressors, the company's specialties. As an apprentice, I began in the paint department and earned thirty cents an hour, $12.00 for a forty-hour week. It doesn't sound like much according to today's standards, but it was double what any of my friends were making. One of my close friends, for example, made $5.00 a week working in a grocery store. As an apprentice, I could anticipate being transferred in a few weeks from the paint department to other departments where I would learn to operate the various kinds of machines used by Gardner-Denver to turn out its products.

About the same time that I began working at Gardner-Denver, Germany invaded Poland, and England and France finally declared war on Germany. Was it possible, I wondered, for the United States to be drawn into war again as it was in World War I? I certainly hoped not, and considering the prevalent anti-war sentiment, I didn't think it would happen. As our relations with Japan deteriorated over the next two years, however, I began to wonder what might develop. Surely, though, a small, inferior country like Japan wouldn't dare to risk a war with us, would it?

The answer came on December 7, 1941, with the surprise attack on Pearl Harbor. A friend, Art Wich, was visiting me when we heard the news on the radio that Sunday afternoon. That was Art's twenty-first birthday, and his reaction was a disgusted, "What a birthday present!" Single and unemployed, he could envision himself being drafted in the near future, and Art was not the kind to adapt well to army regimentation. As an employee of a factory turning out equipment for the armed services, I was deferred.

After leaving the paint department and progressing from drill presses to milling machines to turret lathes, my financial situation improved. Even though I was just an apprentice, the company allowed me occasionally to do piecework jobs, which meant that my pay was based on the number of pieces I produced. I probably averaged $18-20 a week, and I even went a little over $25 on rare occasions.

About a year after I began working at Gardner-Denver, another apprentice, Frank Blaesing, and I met and became close friends and frequently went out together, either by ourselves or with dates. Not long after Pearl Harbor, Frank told me about hearing that the Rock Island Arsenal, at Rock Island, Illinois, about 150 miles north of Quincy, was hiring machinists and suggested that we look into it. We found that we could make $.75 an hour without piecework. In fact, there was no piecework at the arsenal. It sounded like enough of an improvement over our apprenticeship that we decided to submit applications and hope that Gardner-Denver would release us from our apprentice contracts if we were hired. We knew of one apprentice who had been released to go to work at the arsenal, so we thought our chances were good.

About the middle of January, 1942, I was hired and obtained my release from the apprentice contract that I had signed. Frank had not yet been contacted by the arsenal, but we were confident that he soon would be. The day before I was to start work at the arsenal, Mother and I drove in my 1932 Plymouth convertible to Rock Island; and while I was undergoing a physical exam, filling out forms and being familiarized with the department were I would be operating a milling machine, Mother scanned the "For Rent" section of the newspaper and found an ad for a room in a private home that sounded promising. It was much more common then than now for families to rent a spare room to supplement the family income. We found the address, looked at the room and rented it with the understanding that Frank would share the room after being hired. We would each pay $9.00 a week for room and board and would eat all our meals with the family. The room wasn't fancy—just a double bed, adequate storage space for our clothes and personal items, and a table for my combination radio and record player—but it suited us quite well. The bed was comfortable, and the food turned out to be excellent. I even learned to like liver, which until then had been at the top of my "Foods I Love to Hate" list. In fact, it became one of my favorites, much to my mother's surprise. About two weeks after I began work, Frank was hired and joined me.

Working at the arsenal as a machinist was a major improvement over being an apprentice at my former place of employment. It was a relief not to have to depend on piecework to earn a little extra money above the meager apprentice's pay. Moreover, our pay was boosted by the overtime we were required to put in. We worked thirteen days consecutively, with only one day off every other weekend. We were paid time and a half for Saturdays, double time for Sundays, which gave me a paycheck of $90 every two weeks, double what I had made as an apprentice. In 1942 that was a good salary for a 21-year-old. With gas selling for 15-20¢ a gallon and admission to a movie costing only 25¢, a dollar went a long ways. I found myself able to bank nearly half of each pay check. Moreover, we enjoyed the Tri-Cities area of Rock Island and Moline, Illinois, and Davenport, Iowa, which offered much more in the way of entertainment than our hometown.

Some of the better-known big bands occasionally played in Davenport. The only two which I remember are Ted Weems, with whom Perry Como got his start, and Dick Jurgens. The local girls were friendly, so dates were readily available. A blonde Norwegian girl, Gerda, whom I met at a drive-in root beer stand, became one of my favorites.

There was one problem, however. Everyone at the arsenal worked a swing shift: one month on days, one on the 4:00-12:00 shift, and one on the 12:00-8:00 shift. The day shift was fine, of course, and we didn't mind the 12:00-8:00 one too much, for we had ample time to go to a movie or spend some time with a girl friend before going to work. The 4:00-12:00 shift, though, was another matter. During the day there wasn't much to do except go to a movie, and that soon got old. As young, single males we would much rather have had our evenings free to date or go out with friends. Also, although we liked the extra money, working thirteen days in a row became quite a drag after a few months.

On the weekend that we had the day off, Frank and I always drove to Quincy, even though it had to be a rather quick trip. If we were

16

working the 4:00-12:00 shift, we would head for Quincy after getting off at midnight on Friday and return to Rock Island in time to go to work at 4:00 PM Sunday. The other two shifts worked in a similar way so that we always had an evening in Quincy to spend with a girlfriend or other friends. The trips home were almost a necessity in order to get our laundry done by our mothers. There were no laundromats back then, and our rent did not include the use of a washing machine. Even if it had, we would not have been inclined to use it.

As a patriotic twenty-one-year-old, I found myself feeling increasingly uncomfortable about accepting a deferment because of my job and was quite sensitive to the barrage of appeals being made by the various branches of the armed services. I began thinking about the possibility of enlisting. When Frank, therefore, in early September said that he had had his fill of the arsenal grind, we decided to investigate what opportunities the Navy might offer us. The officer at the Navy Recruiting Station assured us that by taking a training course for aviation machinist's mate, we could each be a third class petty officer in about six months. We then agreed that we would return to Quincy, take three or four weeks of vacation, and then enlist in the Navy. On giving the matter further thought, we wondered if we should explore other options. Newsreels we had seen of ships being badly damaged or sunk in naval battles dampened our enthusiasm about going with the Navy. We concluded that the Coast Guard might offer a better chance of surviving the war. A trip to its recruiting office revealed that the Coast Guard could also make use of our machinist skills, so we switched our loyalties from the Navy to the Coast Guard. A major consideration for me was that I knew my mother would not be at all happy about my decision to enlist and thought that the Coast Guard might cause her the least worry. I knew also that she would be more easily reconciled to my enlisting if she believed it was an alternative to being drafted into the infantry. Hence, in a letter that I wrote my parents about my decision to quit my job and enlist, I stretched the truth a little by writing that deferments were no longer being given to the younger employees. The truth was that some were and some were not being deferred, with the latter becoming more and more common. An acquaintance from Quincy who also worked at the arsenal had recently been reclassified

1A, which meant that he was subject to being drafted in the near future, Frank and I informed our foremen at the arsenal of our enlistment plans and said goodbye to the friends we had made in Rock Island. I made a trip to the root beer stand where Gerda worked and promised to write. Then after throwing our few belongings into the rumble seat of my somewhat road-weary 1932 Plymouth convertible, we headed down the road to Quincy. We were concerned about the 150-mile trip because my tires were quite worn. Tires were among the items rationed to aid the war effort, although if I had remained at the arsenal for a while longer, I could probably have obtained a permit for a set of either new tires or retreads, since employees at essential industries like the arsenal had to have transportation. Dad, for example, was able to get retreads throughout the war because his factory produced equipment used by the armed forces. Frank and I, however, were too anxious to get home to delay separating ourselves from the arsenal, and we thought my tires would get us to Quincy. Nevertheless, we were quite relieved when we pulled into town without mishap.

This was the first time off I'd had since going to work shortly after graduating from high school a little over three years ago, and I intended to make the most of it. I thoroughly enjoyed being back home with Mother and Dad and being part of the frequent family get-togethers with my maternal grandparents (my Grandmother VanBlair died in 1934) and Mother's sister and two brothers and their spouses. My worn tires obligingly saw me through the next few weeks of socializing with friends and frequent double dating with Frank. Dad and I again resumed our Saturday fishing trips together, and during the week I occasionally went with my grandfather to a well-stocked private lake to which he had access and which provided excellent bass fishing. The days flew by.

About the middle of October, an acquaintance whom I remember only as Buck (a derivative of his last name, Buckley) came by to tell me that he had heard that the Army Air Forces[1] was offering to place enlistees in schools where they could learn to apply their civilian

---

[1] What is now the United States Air Force, or USAF, was the United States Army Air Forces, commonly referred to as the AAF, during WW II. The plural form *Forces* was used because it encompassed more than one air force, such as the 8th Air Force in England and the 15th Air Force in Italy. It was also frequently called by its previous name, the Army Air Corps.

skills. Buck had also worked at the Arsenal as a machinist and had quit about the same time as Frank and I. I told Frank that I intended to look into the AAF, but he decided to stick with the Coast Guard. After a chat with the Air Forces recruiting officer, Buck and I both enlisted with the understanding that, after completing basic training, we would be sent to armorers school, where we would learn to service the armament on the various kinds of planes used by the Air Forces. Thus, I became the first of my group of close friends to enlist. I almost waited too long, for two or three days after signing up with the AAF, I received a notice to report to my draft board. Had I received that notice prior to enlisting, I would have probably wound up in the infantry.

On November 2, 1942, Mother and Dad accompanied me to the Quincy depot, where I was to board the train for the three-hour trip to the induction center at Peoria, Illinois. I had never seen Dad shed a single tear, even at the death of his mother in 1934, and could not conceive of his not always having complete control of his emotions; however, when I said goodbye to them at the depot, tears were rolling down his cheeks as well as Mother's. I tried to swallow the lump in my throat as I turned and boarded the train. Buck and I found a seat together, then waved goodbye to our parents as the train pulled away from the station. I did not know what Buck was thinking, but I was more than a little apprehensive about what I had let myself in for. I was thankful for the months I had spent working away from home at the arsenal, for I thought that I would at least not be a victim of homesickness.

# CHAPTER 3: FROM K.P. TO WINGS

The next morning found me standing in one line after another with men of assorted shapes and sizes, all of us wearing nothing but our shoes and socks and carrying a basket containing our clothes. One doctor checked my heart; the next one checked for hernias, and others checked various parts of my anatomy. Since I was six feet tall and weighed a scant 125 pounds, some of my relatives were sure that I would flunk the physical; however, I passed it with no problem and became enlistee #16076061. Realistically, there was never any doubt about my passing it. As the saying went, if you could breathe you were in, and I was breathing. An acquaintance who accompanied Buck and me to Peoria had a back deformity that we were sure would get him rejected; however, he was sworn in with us. He was, though, given a medical discharge after only a month of basic training, the last week of which he spent in the base hospital because of back problems.

From Peoria we were sent by train to Scott Field, Illinois, located near Belleville, about 150 miles southeast of Quincy. Here we were issued our uniforms and other equipment, given a haircut (a burr was not mandatory, much to our relief, in spite of what we had heard), and initiated into the army routine. Buck and I were assigned to the same barracks and were able to get adjacent cots. The first morning after our arrival we were routed out of bed before daylight, lined up outside while we shivered through roll call, and then marched to the mess hall for breakfast. Already I had decided that perhaps working thirteen days in a row at the arsenal was not so bad after all.

Later that day after getting into our uniforms (I hated the feel of the wool collar around my neck), we were given time to go to the post office, box up our civilian clothes, and mail them home. Almost certainly the same question was in each man's mind: how long would it be before we could again dress in "civvies"? At that point of the war, the initial optimistic belief that Japan could be quickly defeated had dissipated; thus, I knew that my time in that itchy uniform would be a matter of years, not months.

Incidentally, all the jokes I had heard about men being issued ill-fitting clothes turned out not to be based on fact. The men that I dealt with in Supply took the time to fit me properly, from cap down to shoes.

The day after being issued our uniforms my group was marched to a nearby building, where we took a standardized test. My score of 128 was substantially above the minimum required to apply for the three-month Officer Candidate School, and during the next several weeks, I occasionally thought about submitting an application, especially after having been assigned some disagreeable duty. However, I always decided against doing so. One reason was that I was reluctant to leave the friends I had made; another was that I didn't think I wanted to take on the responsibility. I had a bit of an inferiority complex that I didn't overcome until after I had been in service for a few more months and found myself able to handle everything just as well as anyone else. Another consideration was that we frequently referred to the second lieutenants who were graduates of O.C.S. as ninety-day wonders, and I didn't think I wanted that derogatory term applied to me by the enlisted men whom I might be supervising.

I had been a G.I. for only three days before my name was posted for K.P. duty for Saturday and Sunday. Getting that duty during the week would have been bad enough, but spending the weekend on K.P. when I could have gone into Belleville was a little much! I was awakened before daylight Saturday morning and spent the day doing such disagreeable tasks as scrubbing pots and pans, putting dishes through the dishwasher, wiping off tables, and scrubbing the mess hall floor. During my first few months in service I developed such a distaste for anything associated with kitchens that for many years after my discharge I found it difficult to volunteer for any duty linked to that room.

Sunday morning the routine began all over again. Then, about the middle of the morning, notice came that my parents were there to visit me. Notice was also given that there was no way I could be released from K.P. obligation; however, no objection would be raised to my finding a substitute to pull my duty. With the permission of the mess sergeant, I made a quick trip to my barracks, where one of the guys agreed to sub for me for $5.00, money well spent, I thought.

I quickly exchanged my fatigues for my Class A uniform and double-timed to the waiting room by the main gate to greet Mother and Dad and Uncle Charlie, my mother's brother, who came with them. As we drove the few miles to downtown St. Louis, just across the Mississippi River from Belleville, to eat lunch, I explained how their unexpected visit had got me out of the hated K.P. duty. When we returned to the car after lunch, a policeman was standing by it preparing to write out a ticket. We had parked a little too close to a no parking sign that none of us had seen because it was fastened about ten feet high on a utility pole. After telling us off for not being more observant, he walked off without giving us a ticket. We spent the rest of the afternoon at the Missouri Botanical Gardens, then drove back downtown for dinner. Since Dad and Charlie both had to work the next day, they then dropped me off by the main entrance to Scott Field and drove off. I wasn't homesick, but I had experienced enough of the military life that I fervently wished I could have been going with them. After all, getting K.P. after just a few days in the AAF was enough to dim anyone's patriotism just a little.

After a week at Scott Field, Buck and I were put on a train headed to Kelly Field, just outside of San Antonio, Texas, for basic training. For someone whose longest previous trip had been to the Missouri Ozarks about 200 miles from Quincy, this was quite an experience. I had never eaten or slept on a train before. We were assigned to a Pullman car, and I found the convertible bunks to be quite comfortable. We ate in the diner.

On the morning of the third day after leaving Scott Field, we arrived at San Antonio and were herded off the train. I was a little awestruck at the balmy weather (we were wearing overcoats at Scott Field), the palm trees lining the San Antonio streets and the Southwestern style of architecture that characterized most of the homes that I could see from the back of the truck in which we were transported to Kelly Field. For the first week at Kelly we were restricted to the base while being processed for assignment to a basic training group. As soon as he could, Buck got in touch with a Quincy friend who was stationed at Kelly. His friend Gene, a sergeant, had been in service for about two years and was wise to the ways of the military and Kelly Field. When the weekend came, he insisted that

28

we go with him into San Antonio, where he would even arrange dates for us.

"We can't go to town," Buck said. "We're restricted to base."

"Don't worry about it," Gene replied. "All you have to do is get on the bus and ride into town. There's no checking of passes at the gate. Just make sure that you salute every officer we meet on the street."

Not inclined to be much of a risk taker, I would have much preferred to remain on base until our week's restriction was over. However, not wanting to be labeled chicken, I pretended to think it was a great idea.

Just as Gene had said, there was nothing to it. We carefully saluted every officer as we explored the Alamo and strolled along the San Antonio River. Gene took us to the home of a Mexican family that evening. The house was large and well furnished, and I assumed the father must have a good income. Gene introduced us first to the parents, then to the three daughters, all pretty girls, with whom we spent the evening before returning to base. I had been in service less than two weeks and had already successfully gone AWOL. I breathed a big sigh of relief, however, when we were safely back on base and was not anxious to repeat the experience.

After being assigned to a basic training group, Buck and I were assigned to separate but adjacent quarters. We were housed in structures with wooden floors and six-foot-high sides, about half of which was screen, with canvas that could be rolled down to cover the screen in inclement weather. The roof was canvas. There were several rows of these semi-tents, each of which was perhaps fifteen feet square and comfortably accommodated four single canvas cots. One of the first things we learned was to make a bed tight enough that a quarter would bounce on the top blanket. I couldn't quite see how that would help me be a good soldier, but if the sergeant said to do it, I knew I had better do it.

Once settled into the routine, I found basic training not all that bad except for the K.P. and latrine duty at which each of us had to take his turn. Our days were taken up with lectures, training films, rigorous calisthenics and, of course, many hours of close order drill. We left-faced, right-faced, about-faced, and to-the-rear marched until we could have done it in our sleep. Before long, I found myself enjoying the drilling, for when we were marching, I didn't have to take notes, do much thinking, or listen to boring lectures. It was just a matter of listening and responding to commands.

**The author during basic training at Kelly Field, San Antonio, Texas, in December 1942.**

We frequently found time to play softball, football, and volleyball and had some heated competitions. Except for Saturday mornings, the weekends were ours to come and go as we wished, an improvement on Rock Island, at least. The people of San Antonio were not overly friendly but, from what I was told, now had a much better attitude toward servicemen than before Pearl Harbor. I suppose the infusion of all those Northerners took some getting used to, but the wave of patriotism that followed Pearl Harbor helped them to survive the shock.

About half way through basic training came Christmas, my first away from home, for which Mother and Dad sent me a portable radio that I used until I left for overseas about eleven months later. I thought of my parents back home getting together with Mother's family, exchanging gifts, and enjoying each other's company and very much wished I could be there. After eating our Christmas dinner of turkey and all the trimmings at the mess hall, Buck and I and some friends went into town. The day had begun as an unusually warm day, but during the afternoon the wind shifted to the north and the temperature began dropping. By the time we returned to Kelly Field that evening, it was below freezing and, not having taken overcoats with us, so were we. That was not unusual, we were told, for that part of Texas in the winter months.

Toward the end of December we were assembled for an immunization shot of some kind. As the line slowly moved past the doctor, each man received an injection in the left arm. When my turn came, I turned my head and watched as the doctor jabbed my arm, then withdrew the syringe. However, there was a problem: the needle came loose and remained stuck in my arm. The doctor quickly grabbed it and pulled it out. The mishap did not bother me, but the man immediately behind me grew pale, headed for a nearby chair, and sat with his head lowered. He did not faint, but he obviously was not ready to get his vaccine.

I was under the impression that the Civil War had ended in 1865, but the all-too-numerous Texans in our group seemed to think otherwise. Continual bickering about it went on between them and us Yankees. I wondered sometimes if they realized that this was a different war and that we were now on the same side. That and their, to me, insufferable bragging about Texas left me with an aversion for that state that I have never completely overcome. When Alaska became a state in later years, I was pleased that Texans could no longer brag about theirs being the largest state.

On completing basic training at the end of January, Buck and I were transferred to Buckley Field, a few miles outside of Denver, where we were to attend armorers' school. While here, we would learn to install and service the armament on fighter planes. The school operated twenty-four hours a day so that three different groups of men could be run through at the same time. Our group had the four-to-twelve shift. Since all students were permitted to go into Denver only on weekends, our spending evenings in class was not a major concern.

Instead of the semi-tents of our basic training days, we now were housed in one-story wood barracks with furnaces. Buck and I were in the same building and were assigned cots that were close together, although not side by side. When we arrived, the weather was cold, damp and dreary, and the sheepskin-lined coats we were issued on arrival felt good. It was quite a change from San Antonio, where we had seldom used the oil stoves in our semi-tents except during the occasionally cool nights.

During the few days between our arrival at Buckley and the start of our classes, my name was posted for a day of K.P. I was beginning to wonder if the AAF always started at the end of the alphabet and wished my name were Morris or Nash so that it might be more obscurely placed in the middle. Just as we were completing the clean-up after the noon meal, the wind began to blow quite hard and a dust storm ensued. It did not last long, but even though all doors and windows were kept closed, everything was covered with a fine layer of dust. We had to give the mess hall a complete cleaning—mop the floor, wash off all tables and other furnishings, and wash every dish, pot and pan. Ordinary K.P. was bad enough, but this was a little too much.

In late February Mother wrote that she was taking the train to Denver for a brief visit. She would arrive Friday night and depart Monday morning so as to be there during my weekend time off from class. Since bus transportation into Denver was not available when we finished class at midnight, I set my alarm to awaken me at 6:00 Saturday morning, hurriedly shaved and dressed, caught the bus into town, and was knocking on her hotel room door in time to have breakfast with her. I learned that she had come with a Quincy friend whose husband was also going through school at Buckley. Although we didn't do much besides visit the state capital building and go through some of the large downtown stores, where Mother did a little shopping, the two days went by quickly, and it was time for me to report back to base for my 4:00 P.M. class on Sunday.

I had explained to Mother that I could not see her off Monday morning because we were restricted to base during the week, which she understood and had no problem with.  When the corporal in charge of our barracks heard of the situation after I returned Sunday afternoon, he called me aside and said something like this:

"I know you'd like to see your mother off tomorrow morning, but you know that I can't give you your pass.  However, I keep the passes on that ledge by my bunk, and yours will be on top.  If you want to take it while I'm still sleeping Monday morning and head for town, there should be no problem.  Just be sure you're back in plenty of time to make the four o'clock formation.  It is highly unlikely that you will run into any problem, but if you do get caught, just remember that I did not give you the pass."  I assured him that I would accept full responsibility if anything untoward happened.

For the second time in my brief Air Forces career, I made a successful AWOL excursion. Mother readily accepted my explanation that I had obtained permission to leave the base (in one sense I had, since it was the corporal's idea), and I did not tell her otherwise until some time later. I knew the chances of anything going wrong were negligible but, nevertheless, was relieved to get back to my barracks. That was my last unauthorized expedition off a base during my time in service.

Occupying the cot next to mine was a short (about five feet, four inches) Italian from Boston by the name of Albert Spadafora, whom everyone quite naturally addressed as Shorty. My first impression of him was somewhat negative—he seemed a little too cocky. That first impression was faulty, however, and before long we were close friends. Also in our barracks was Steve, whose full name was Horace Stephens—for some reason, we frequently went by a form of our last name; for example, I was Van to most friends. With such a given name, he probably preferred being called Steve. He was a native of Peoria who had gone through basic training in my group but whom I had previously known only casually. He, too, now became a good friend; and Steve, Shorty, Buck and I usually made a foursome on weekends in Denver. We usually made the Brass Rail our first stop. It was a night club popular with servicemen and, because of the numerous servicemen, single girls. We soon found that sticking together made it more difficult to pick up girls because most of them seemed to travel in twos. Therefore, we began splitting into pairs after arriving at the Brass Rail and found that our success rate showed a marked improvement. When I look back at the drinking and night clubbing I did during my three years in the AAF, I'm not at all pleased with myself. Much to my parents' satisfaction, I quit both when I met my wife-to-be about eight months after my discharge.

On March 20 we finished armorers school and sewed on the PFC stripes that came with graduation. About two weeks prior to that, Shorty had told me about seeing an announcement on the bulletin board that volunteers were wanted for aerial gunnery school and urged me to sign up together with him and Steve. I was not too sure at first if I wanted to expose myself to the probability of being shot at while 20,000-25,000 feet in the air. However, one incentive was an automatic promotion to sergeant on completion of gunnery school, which meant a substantial increase in pay and privileges—no more K.P.! Also, I remembered a brief film by Jimmy Stewart promoting the Air Forces that I had seen at a movie in Rock Island. He made flying sound quite glamorous and implied that wings on a uniform always attracted the girls. The main factor, however, was my close friendship with Shorty and Steve. It didn't take much persuasion on their part for me to accompany them to the headquarters building to sign up. Since Buck preferred the ground, he did not volunteer, and so our journey together in the AAF ended, and I began the next leg with Shorty and Steve.

When I wrote Mother and Dad about aerial gunnery school, I left the impression that I had no choice in the matter, for I knew they would not approve of their only son's volunteering for something that was certain to lead to his being exposed to enemy fire. I figured they would better reconcile themselves to it if they thought I had been more or less drafted for the school. They did not find out otherwise until after I returned home following my discharge, when I unthinkingly referred to my volunteering for aerial gunnery school. Mother immediately picked up on my slip of the tongue: "I thought you said you had no choice about gunnery school!" I had to explain why I handled it as I did.

The end of March found Shorty, Steve, and me beginning our gunnery training at HAGS (Harlingen Aerial Gunnery School) near Harlingen, Texas, not far from the Gulf of Mexico and the Mexican border. Once again I experienced a radical change in climate. We packed our wool uniforms away and got out our summer khakis. Most of us referred to the school by using the acronym HAGS, a practice that some of the WACs (Women's Army Corps) who worked there took as a kind of personal affront.

I liked the HAGS base. All the barracks were neat, white, two-story frame buildings. All had single cots with foot lockers and tables for writing letters or playing cards. The interiors provided more space than I was used to. Our day room (recreation building) provided a pool table and magazines. A theater showed up-to-date movies, and books could be checked out from a central library. The food was superior to that provided at either Kelly or Buckley Fields, and wonder of wonders, I did not have to do K.P. during my stay at HAGS!

During the next several weeks we learned how to operate the various gun turrets used on bombers, estimate distance and lead (electric eye guns were helpful here), identify Allied and enemy aircraft by their silhouettes, disassemble and assemble a machine gun while we were blindfolded, and correct various kinds of malfunctions in a machine gun. Since we did not know at this point which position we would be assigned to after joining a combat crew, we absorbed all we could about each turret. Most of the foregoing areas were covered in classroom instruction. We also shot numerous rounds of skeet and trap, the purpose of which was to make leading a target a matter of habit. Never having used a shotgun before, I missed far more of the clay pigeons than I hit at first; however, I gradually improved until I broke 22 of 25 birds for my high score in a round of skeet. Far more challenging was trying to hit clay pigeons as we stood in the back of a moving truck. As the truck was driven around a large circle, the discs were released at various angles. All of us missed more than we hit, which our instructor seemed to expect, since he did not criticize our performance.

The daily calisthenics were far more rigorous than I had previously encountered in either basic training or armorers school. As I recall, we took 30-45 minutes of calisthenics daily, which always concluded with pushups. Our instructor kept increasing the number we were required to do until by the end of the three months of school I found myself able to do thirty without becoming overly tired. I had now gone from a skinny 125 pounds to a more respectable 145 and had added muscle. After calisthenics we ran. At first, even though we ran just a few blocks, I quickly became winded. As we continued to run, however, that problem disappeared even though the distance of our runs was gradually increased. For the first time in my few months of service, I found myself actually enjoying the calisthenics and running.

We spent one week on the firing range, which was located several miles from the main base in a desolate area within hiking distance of the Gulf. Much of our time here was occupied in shooting with a machine gun at a moving ground target and fixing gun malfunctions. One afternoon the non-com in charge of our group took us on a hike to the Gulf for a swim. Because it was hot, I foolishly look off my shirt while we hiked and suffered a painful sunburn on my back and shoulders. For the next few nights I slept on my stomach. Some of the men delighted in coming up behind me and giving me a little pat on the back just to see me cringe.

One of the fellows in our group was the only one I ever met who made an art of shining shoes. He could take a pair of G.I. shoes and make them shine like polished brass. Several of us tried to get the same results but, while we could get a good shine, never matched his product. Several of the men even paid him to shine their shoes.

Finally the ground phase of our training was completed, and the much-anticipated aerial phase began. Our initial flight, the purpose of which was to give us an idea of what it was like to fly (none of us had ever been in a plane), was in a small transport plane. It was a gloomy, overcast day, and when we emerged into the brilliant sunlight reflecting off the billowy, white clouds, I was astonished at how beautiful it was. I was hooked on flying; I loved it. I never became airsick and, unlike some of the men, didn't mind taking off and landing.

During the next two weeks, each of us went up several times in an AT-6 and fired at a target towed by another plane. The AT-6 was a single-engine monoplane with two cockpits, the back one of which was occupied by the student gunner, who fired at the target with a machine gun mounted on a post similar to the way an oar is mounted on a boat. I was never informed about how well I had done. I assumed that if I hadn't scored enough hits, I would have been notified and assigned some extra practice.

Many of the second lieutenants who flew the planes for us were unhappy with their assignment and wished to complete their flights as quickly as possible. Since we were required to fire a specified number of rounds, if a gun malfunctioned and could not be fixed in the air, the pilot had to land so that the student could mount another gun on the post, then take him back up to fire the rest of his ammunition. Some of the pilots, therefore, when a malfunction occurred, would tell the student gunner to throw the unused ammunition over the side. Since all firing was done over the Gulf, there was little danger of the unused ammunition being discovered and exposing the deception. When one of the men in our barracks, who had a reputation of being a little dense, had his gun to malfunction, the pilot shouted, "Throw it over the side." The student promptly picked up both gun and ammunition and dropped it all over the side. Needless to say, he did not finish gunnery school. I never heard what, if anything, happened to the pilot.

After being based near San Antonio and Denver, I found Harlingen and nearby Brownsville to be rather dull towns, offering little in the way of entertainment other than movies. Dates were hard to get; in fact, none of my friends or I managed to line up a single date during our time at HAGS.

On one of our trips into Brownsville, we decided to splurge on dinner at a rather expensive restaurant. I thought the waitress looked a little quizzical when I ordered a dozen fried oysters, and when she brought the order I found out why. The oysters were huge, at least twice the size of those I was used to eating at home. I had no idea oysters grew that big. I wasn't about to act surprised, however, and made no comment as I waded through them. They were quite good.

About two weeks before each class finished training, it was the custom for the base to give the students a day off and furnish bus transportation to Matamoros, a Mexican city just across the border. The contrast between Matamoros and the American towns of Harlingen and Brownsville was remarkable, even though the latter two both had a large Mexican population. This was my first contact with a culture radically different from my own, and it was an eye opener.

Matamoros was a dirty town, both physically and morally, so much so that I am surprised that the Air Forces encouraged our spending a day there. Vulgar shows of one kind or another abounded, and prostitution was quite openly promoted. As we left the bus, we were met by little Mexican boys asking, "Wanna meet my sister (they pronounced it *seester*)?" For someone such as I who was still not too wise in the ways of the world in spite of six months in service, it was a bit of a culture shock. The closest I came to doing anything of which my mother would not approve was drinking a shot of tequila, together with Shorty and Steve, just to see what it tasted like. One was more than enough! Although I was glad to have experienced a day in Old Mexico, I was not anxious to repeat the trip. One day in Matamoros was enough to last me a lifetime.

**Photo taken when the author graduated from Harlingen Aerial Gunnery School in May 1943.**

Graduation from gunnery school on May 15, 1943, was the highlight of my time in service until then. It meant pinning on the coveted pair of wings, sewing on sergeant's stripes (goodbye, K.P.!) and being issued the special gear for flying personnel, including the leather A-2 jackets that distinguished flight from ground personnel, the heavy fleece-lined high altitude suits, and nice B4 flight bags in which to pack our gear. Those wings on the left side of my chest made me feel as if I had become someone a little special. We sweated under the hot Texas sun as we put on the high altitude suits and took

47

each other's pictures to send home to impress wives, parents and other

family members and girl friends.

# CHAPTER 4: THE ALFRED H. LOCKE CREW

From Harlingen Shorty and I (Steve accepted an opportunity to remain as an instructor) took another train ride, this time to Salt Lake City. I found the train rides that accompanied transfers from one base to another to be an enjoyable break from the army routine. With no duties to perform, we had two or three days in which to watch the scenery go by, talk, read, sleep, write letters, and either watch or sit in on the poker game that ceased only for meals and converting of the seats into beds. I frequently watched the poker players but did not participate; Shorty, on the other hand, frequently played. Arrival at the next base, consequently, was not an eagerly anticipated event, since it meant a return to the military way of life. I always traveled in Pullmans with porters to make up the berths. I don't know if men in the other branches of the armed services usually traveled as comfortably as we did, but the AAF seemed to want us to be well taken care of in this respect. The one drawback to those train trips was the soot that the steam engine put out. It was a special problem in summer when we had the windows open. Even with the windows closed, the soot seemed to collect around our necks. On arriving at our destination, we showered as quickly as possible.

The typical allotment for travel meals was $1.00 for those taken in the diner, 75c for others, according to the travel orders that I saved. Since troop trains did not have diners—at least, none that I was on except for our trip from Scott Field to Kelly Field—the trains stopped at meal time at some town where arrangements had been made for us to eat in a nearby restaurant, which frequently was a Harvey Restaurant in the town's depot. The Harvey chain of restaurants has gone the way of the steam locomotive, but during WW II and for many years previously, as well, a Harvey could be found in many depots throughout the country. Many of the scenes of "The Harvey Girls," starring Judy Garland, had the town's Harvey Restaurant as their setting.

At Salt Lake City we took three weeks of intensive training in turret operation. In a letter to my parents written after the first day, I complained, "We've got the toughest top sergeant here that I've ever run in to. He really told us what was what when we started school. He has a very fluent vocabulary when it comes to strong language."

The impression he made was short-lived, for I now have no recollection of him whatsoever. In the same letter, I wrote, "This school is located on the Salt Lake City fair grounds, and our barracks used to be where they had exhibits. There are about 600 men in here, so you can see how much privacy I have." I didn't much like it but figured I could tolerate it for three weeks. Shorty and I went into Salt Lake City on Sunday, the only day we had free, but once we had seen such things as the Temple, there was little to do. Salt Lake City on Sunday offered little in the way of the kind of entertainment a G.I. would be looking for—no open bars and little opportunity to meet girls.

The school ran a day and a night shift. I was one of the lucky ones to be placed in the day shift, but Shorty drew the night one. Thus, we didn't see much of one another during the three-week school except on Sunday. Several men, however, whom I had known since our Buckley Field days were with me in the day shift, so I had friends available. According to a card in my scrapbook, I completed the course with a grade of 96.

Our next stop on June 22 was Gowen Field at Boise, Idaho, to await assignment to a combat group. On July 6 I was pleasantly surprised to receive a telegram from Dad saying that he would arrive at 1:50 P.M. on July 8. When I asked how he was able to get time off, since his factory was primarily handling government contracts, he explained that men wanting to visit their sons or daughters in service were allowed to take time off to do so. Because we were merely awaiting assignment and had few duties, I was able to get a pass covering the three days he stayed, with the provision that I check the bulletin board daily for any announcements concerning me. Since I was allowed to stay in town each evening, we shared a hotel room. I didn't even have to go AWOL in order to go with him when the time came for him to board the train to go home.

Through the years one of Dad's favorite stories involved his train trip to Boise. Trains were very crowded during the war, and passengers took seats wherever they could find them. Dad wound up in the men's room compartment sitting next to a man who ate garlic with each meal. It was almost more than Dad could take.

Shorty and I requested assignment to the same crew, and on July 18 we received orders assigning us to the newly formed 448th Heavy Bombardment Group, 715th Squadron, flying the four-engine B-24 Liberator. We could now anticipate being on flying status in a few days, which meant drawing an additional fifty percent of our base pay as flight pay. Since I had no food, rent or clothing expenses, I would be as well off financially as when I was working at the arsenal. Things were looking up!

Two days later Shorty and I arrived at Wendover Field in Utah at the Nevada border. On stepping off the train at the little town of Wendover, I was disappointed by what I saw. Wendover and our base were in the middle of a huge expanse of salt flats, with no trees and little vegetation of any kind. It was desolate. There was so little to Wendover that we rarely bothered to go there in our off-duty hours. It made Harlingen look like a thriving metropolis. About the only attraction in Wendover was its tavern that straddled the Utah/Nevada border. Because Utah was a dry state, the bar had to be located on the Nevada side of the building.

On getting acquainted with the other members of our crew, Shorty and I were much impressed by our pilot, Lt. Herrick. He made flying a B-24 look easy. Unfortunately, he was with us for only a short time. A minor heart problem showed up, and he was grounded. Our replacement pilot was Lt. Al Locke, a native of Oklahoma, who at first lacked some of Lt. Herrick's touch with the Liberator but who very quickly developed into an excellent pilot. He had a good sense of humor, was never one to "pull rank" on the enlisted men of his crew and, moreover, took good care of us. As soon as possible, he recommended us for promotion to staff sergeant (the gunners) and tech sergeant (engineer and radio operator). I liked him very much and, even more important, I trusted him. I quickly developed complete confidence that, once we began flying combat missions, he would get us back to our base as long as we still had an engine running.

The Alfred H. Locke crew. *Top row, left to right:* Lt. Arthur Delclisur,
bombardier: Lt. Alfred H. Locke, pilot; Lt. Errol Self, co-pilot; Lt. John
Hortenstine, navigator. *Bottom row, left to right:* Sgt. Virgil Carrol,
engineer/top turret; Sgt. Pedro (Pete) Paez, asst. engineer /waist gunner; Sgt.
Albert (Shorty) Spadafora, ball turret: Sgt. Frank (Cappy) Cappello, radio
operator; Sgt. Henry (Hank) Boisclair, waist gunner; Sgt. Dale vanBlair, tail
turret/asst. radio operator.

Lt. Al Locke, the crew's pilot, and his wife, Patricia.

The other seven members of our ten-man crew were the following: Lt. Errol Self, co-pilot, from California; Lt. John Hortenstine, navigator, from Virginia; Lt. Arthur Delclisur, bombardier, from Brooklyn; Sgt. Virgil Carrol, engineer and top turret gunner, from Brooklyn; Sgt. Frank Cappello, radio operator, from Brooklyn; Sgt. Pedro (Pete) Paez, assistant engineer and left waist gunner, from California; and Sgt. Henry (Hank) Boisclair, from Florida, right waist gunner. Shorty was ball turret gunner, and I was tail gunner. Our crew and eleven others that accompanied us from Gowen Field to Wendover were among the first to be assigned to the 448th.

Many crews had eighteen- and nineteen-year-old members. We did not. Frank Cappello (he very quickly became "Cappy"), who I think was twenty, was the youngest. Pete and Hank, who were in their lower thirties, were the oldest. The rest of us were in our low twenties. At twenty-two, I was a year older than our pilot, Lt. Locke. Five of our crew, more than on most crews, were married: Lt. Locke, Lt. Self, Virgil, Pete and Hank.

Lt. Self was a full-blooded Apache Indian, very handsome, and had been a dancer in Hollywood. I saw him in a brief appearance in a musical film after the war. Lt. Delclisur was a very considerate, kind person and turned out to be an excellent bombardier. After our crew had been together for a few weeks, he began to frequently single me out to talk to when our crew met to fly a practice mission or for some other reason, and I felt that we could have become close friends had it not been for military protocol. Lt. Hortenstine was a top-notch navigator. Because all of our officers gained recognition as being among the best, we later were tapped to become a lead crew after flying eight missions.

**The author's close friend, Albert Spadafora, nicknamed Shorty.**

All of our crew's enlisted men were also very reliable, well trained, and efficient. Virgil Carrol, our engineer, was one of the best, if not the best, in our squadron and was probably just as important a factor in our becoming a lead crew as were our officers. He knew the B-24 about as well as anyone could, and I was confident in his ability to solve any mechanical problems that might arise. Pete Paez was Mexican, short and a little on the chunky side, and had an engaging personality. He liked people and people liked him. We were a very compatible group and I was never aware of a disagreement among any two of us. I liked them all, but the bond between Shorty and me was especially strong. We were inseparable; where one was, the other was likely to be. Virgil and Pete frequently accompanied Shorty and me when we went into whatever town was near the base where we happened to be stationed, but Frank (Cappy) Cappello and Henry (Hank) Boisclair rarely went with us. Each seemed to prefer to go alone.

Regarding assignment of gunners to the turrets and waist guns, standard procedure was for the engineer to man the top turret, since his duties required that he be in the cockpit area, and for the bombardier to man the nose turret except on the bomb run, when he had to operate the bomb sight. When we had our initial meeting after arriving at Wendover, Lt. Herrick left it up to the gunners to decide who would fill the other positions. Shorty's size made him a natural for the ball turret, the most cramped of all the turrets, which he was quite willing to do. When I expressed a preference for the tail turret, Pete and Hank said that they didn't want to fly in that turret anyway and preferred to man the waist guns. Thus, each gunner wound up at the position which he preferred without any controversy.

The tail turret on the B-24 was manufactured by Consolidated Aircraft and was hydraulically operated. Before entering the turret, the gunner had to make sure that the shut-off valve was in the off position; otherwise, an accidental movement of the control handle could cause the turret to rotate and pin the gunner between the edge of the door and the edge of the fuselage. Once inside, the gunner then opened the shut-off valve and used the control handles to move both turret and guns. The turret could be moved from side to side and the guns up and down simultaneously so that it was possible to track an enemy plane with the two .50 caliber machine guns regardless of its angle or direction of flight. Hydraulic stops kept the turret from being rotated so far that the guns would strike any part of the tail section. A plexiglass dome that covered the top front half provided about a 180-degree field of vision. At the front of the turret, a slightly angled slab of laminated armor glass provided protection and also let the gunner see fighters that might be attacking from behind or below his position. The turret had sliding doors that could be closed behind the gunner; however, I always left my doors open so that I could get out quickly in case of an emergency. I found the padded seat to be reasonably comfortable and had no problem fitting my six-foot frame into the turret.

Most of our training was done in the B-24D, which had a "greenhouse" nose rather than a nose turret. A few weeks before we went overseas, we were assigned a B-24H, which had a nose turret. Although the B-24 Liberator did not get the publicity received by the B-17, I was quite satisfied to be assigned to it, particularly as a tail gunner, for from what I knew about the B-17's tail turret, it was quite cramped. The Liberator was a little faster, carried a heavier bomb load, and had a longer range than the B-17 Fortress. The bomb bay doors of the B-17 were hinged and swung down when opened, which created substantial air resistance; those on the B-24 rolled up inside the fuselage, thus eliminating much of the drag. The B-24 had a maximum speed of 290 mph and a cruising speed of 215 mph, although we flew our missions at less than that, as I recall, perhaps 150-175. In combat, it would take a lot of punishment and keep on flying, and its four Pratt and Whitney engines were as rugged and dependable as any made, according to Virgil, our engineer. Our last mission was to prove him right. During WW II more B-24s were produced than any other American plane. A modified B-24, by the way, was Winston Churchill's preferred mode of travel.

A not-too-efficient heating system was provided for those flying in the nose of the plane (pilot, co-pilot, navigator, bombardier, engineer and radio operator), but flying at high altitude in the waist (the section behind the wings) of a bomber was not a pleasant experience, particularly with the waist windows open, as they had to be on combat missions. With the wind blowing a gale through the windows at the temperatures encountered at 20,000-25,000 feet, it was COLD. On our practice flights in the States, we usually kept the windows closed at the higher altitudes unless for some reason they had to be kept open. For example, when we were practicing formation flying, those of us in the waist section kept an eye on the planes flying next to us so that if one got a little too close, we could be ready to clip on our chest-pack parachutes in case of a collision.

On our early training flights, Lt. Locke on a few occasions had trouble making smooth landings. The B-24 had a tricycle landing gear and a tail skid. The pilot landed by touching down with the two main landing gear beneath the wings and then bringing the nose down until the nose wheel touched. On one of those early training flights, as I sat on a box during our landing approach, I suddenly felt a jolt, and the box on which I sat lifted several inches, spilling me to the floor. Lt. Locke had come in with the tail skid a little too low, letting the skid hit and forcing it up through the fuselage about a foot. I happened to be sitting directly above the skid. In the following few days, Lt. Locke spent much of his own time making practice landings until he had the technique mastered. He never again had a problem.

Life as a crew member was a welcome change from what I had experienced in my previous months in the Air Forces. When we were not flying, few demands were made on our time. Partly because Wendover Field was in such a desolate area, the daily practice flights were a pleasure, for they were frequently over nearby scenic mountains, a welcome change from the hot, barren salt flats. Since flights at 10,000 feet or higher called for donning oxygen masks and, depending on the temperature, heavy flying suits, I preferred those below that altitude; however, I enjoyed flying regardless of the altitude, as did the others. Those of us who were gunners usually had little to do on practice flights. If we tired of practicing operating our turrets or looking out the waist windows at the landscape below, we stretched out on the floor and slept. At this stage in our training, the war seemed to be rather remote, even though I knew our involvement was inevitable unless something unforeseen happened.

A few miles from Wendover Field was a fair-sized lake. On two or three occasions, Lt. Locke arranged for our crew to be transported to it for a swim after the sun went down (we'd have all been burned to a crisp had we gone while the sun was up, and I had had enough of that in Texas). The water was salty but pleasant in which to swim. Those outings were a pleasant break in the routine.

A month or so after our transfer to Wendover, Pete, Hank, Shorty and I, together with the gunners from all other crews, were sent for two weeks to the gunnery range for a refresher course. The gunnery range was in the foothills of mountains several miles from the main base. While the accommodations at the main base were not fancy, they were far superior to those at the range, where we lived in semi-tents with canvas cots. On the main base we lived in wooden barracks with double bunks that included springs and mattresses. Also, the gunnery range had no PX. I was relieved when the two weeks were up and we returned to the main base and flying.

I thoroughly disliked just one duty that I shared with the other gunners: taking strike photos on practice bombing runs. The photos were taken through the escape hatch in the bottom of the waist section with the hatch cover open, and getting into position to take the photos required extending one's head and shoulders over the opening while holding a large camera. Since a parachute could not be worn because its bulk interfered with getting into position, if the photographer fell through the opening he was done for. Other crew members, therefore, had to hold on to the photographer's legs and feet. Even with them holding on to me, I found looking through the hatch with nothing between my upper body and the earth far below to be a scary experience, as did the other men. No one ever volunteered to take another's turn at the duty. I would have done anything for Shorty except sub for him. After all, even the closest of friendships has its limits!

Early in September 1943, our crew received seven-day furloughs. Thinking it would be fun to surprise our parents, Shorty and I both decided against notifying them that we were coming home. We rode a bus to Salt Lake City, where we had made plane reservations. I boarded a United Airlines plane and flew to St. Louis, then took the train to Quincy. The flight to St. Louis was a stormy, rough one, and many of the passengers got sick. Because of the hours of flying that I had behind me, I had no problem—even felt a little smug, I think, sort of like a professional among amateurs.

On arriving home after a quick taxi ride from the train station, I found the house deserted but the door unlocked (most people never locked their homes back then, at least not in Quincy). Since it was a Sunday afternoon, a time that Mother and Dad frequently got together with other members of Mother's family, I figured I could locate them with a phone call or two. My first call to my Aunt Elsie was all it took. I can still remember the phone conversation word for word after Elsie answered the phone:

"Hi, Elsie. Are Mother and Dad there?"

"Dale! Where are you?"

"I'm home on furlough."

With that Elsie turned and shouted, "Lora! Lora! Dale's home!"

Mother grabbed the phone. "Don't leave! Don't leave! We'll be right home!"

"Don't worry," I said. "I'm not going anywhere." But I think by the time I finished, she and Dad were on their way to the car.

During the few minutes it took them to drive home (Dad was a careful driver, but I suspect he exceeded the speed limit a little on this trip), I walked slowly through the house and went upstairs to my room, where everything was as I had left it about ten months ago, even to the pennies that I had got into the habit of throwing into a little wire basket on my dresser. It was great to be home again! Never before had I appreciated it quite as much as I did then.

As it happened, the whole clan had gathered at Elsie and Roscoe's home that Sunday afternoon, including Grandma and Granddad and Charlie and Howard, Mother's two brothers, and their wives. Mother and Dad arrived home first, with the others not more than a minute behind. It was a grand reunion!

About 11:30 that night Mother and Dad went to bed, and I walked up the stairs to my room. *MY* room! For a few minutes I sat on the edge of the bed and savored the moment. For the next six nights, I wouldn't have to share space with anyone else. I would be sleeping in a comfortable, roomy bed and could get up when I pleased. For breakfast I would have fried eggs served on a china plate instead of a metal tray and a bowl of my favorite cereal, Wheaties. Finally I turned back the sheet, went to bed and almost instantly fell asleep.

I did my best to make the most of every minute of my furlough. There were family gatherings, a fishing trip or two, dating, and *lots of good food.* By a lucky coincidence, two of my closest Quincy friends, Carl Eyre and Ken Plowman (both had been drafted after my enlistment), were also home on leave and still had two days left, so we went out together the next two evenings. The joy of being reunited with family and friends for a week was almost worth having gone into the Air Forces. I had originally intended to drive to Rock Island to visit Gerda, whom I had dated while living there and with whom I had frequently corresponded; however, with only a week of leave, I could not bring myself to take the time away from Mother and Dad.

A night or two after Carl and Ken left, I went to the Elks Club, a nightclub open to the public, by myself, where I ran into a friend who introduced me to her girl friend, Jane (not her real name). Since we hit it off quite well, I dated her each of the remaining two evenings of my leave, which led to our exchanging frequent letters after I left.

As much as I disliked seeing the furlough end, it had to be more difficult for my parents, who knew I would be going overseas before the year was over. In a few months worry would be a continuous part of their lives. Whenever they saw a headline about planes being lost in whatever area our bomb group was serving, they would wonder if ours was one of them until receiving another letter from me. When Sunday came, the day I had to catch my flight back to Salt Lake City, we got up early, and Dad and Mother drove me to the St. Louis airport, about a three-hour trip. When the time came for me to board the plane, I knew they must be wondering if I would come back. As an optimist, I knew that I would. If I had known of the high AAF casualty rate, I might not have been so sure.

**Shorty and his fiancée, Mary Lattanzio, who become engaged on the crew's September 1943 furlough.**

My flight to Salt Lake City was a little late, and I was concerned about arriving in time to catch the bus that would get me to Wendover about an hour before my furlough officially ended at midnight. Fortunately, I made connections and checked into the 715th headquarters a little after 11:00 P.M. Shorty was already in bed and asleep, so I did not get to talk to him until the next morning, when he surprised me with the announcement that he was now engaged. His fiancée was Mary Lattanzio, with whom I would become well acquainted after the war.

Soon after my return from leave, the 448th moved on September 16 to Sioux City, Iowa, to complete its training prior to overseas duty. Sioux City was a good soldier's town. The civilians were hospitable, and dates were easy to come by. Shortly after our arrival, the wives of Lt. Locke and Lt. Self came for a visit, both arriving at the same time, though it was not planned. One morning while the wives were there, Lt. Locke had a big grin on his face when he met us at the plane for a practice flight. The previous evening as Lt. Locke and his wife were returning to their hotel, they had met Self at the elevator in the hotel. He had taken his wife to her room and was going out to meet a local girl. He had told his wife he had to return to the base. That was Lt. Self. He attracted women like honey attracts flies, and he made the most of it. Lt. Locke, on the other hand, was completely true to his wife. He never expressed an interest in anyone other than his wife in my hearing. Of all the married men that I knew during my three years in service, very few were completely faithful to their wives. It wasn't a matter of their not loving their wives; on the contrary, most longed to be reunited with them. However, like the single men, the married ones desired feminine companionship, and "when the cat's away the mice will play." Most married men did not have our pilot's self-discipline.

At Sioux City Shorty began spending quite a bit of his time playing poker or shooting dice, and it seemed to me that more often than not, he came out behind. Consequently, he occasionally borrowed money from me, which was always promptly returned on payday. He finally decided that he would give me most of his money before he got into a game with instructions not to give him any, no matter what he said, until he was safely away. At other times, when I saw that he was ahead, I would find an excuse to take him away from the game, such as "Come on, Shorty. We've got to catch the bus into town." He would usually comply within a few minutes.

A directive from 448th headquarters mandated that each crew should select someone to receive enough training to fill in for the radio operator in case of his being wounded or killed on a mission. I was designated that person for our crew. I devoted many hours to learning the Morse code and going with Cappy to the building where radio operators could practice sending and receiving; however, becoming proficient at using the Morse code required much more practice than I had time for, and I was most thankful I never had to fill in for Cappy after we began combat flying.

On gathering at the plane for one of our practice flights, Lt. Locke surprised me by telling me that he was going to fly us over Quincy, which was less than three hundred air miles away. Had I known his plan ahead of time, I would have called home so that Mother and Dad could have been looking for our B-24. As we circled over my home town twice, I picked out familiar buildings and areas and felt a bit of a temptation to go AWOL via parachute.

On October 22 I received orders promoting me to staff sergeant. My monthly base pay would now be $96, plus 50% flight pay, for a total of $144 a month. Since I had been designated the lead gunner on our crew (the other gunners elected me to that position), I was the first of the gunners to receive the staff rating.[2] The standard procedure was for the head engineer and the radio operator to make tech sergeant; the other enlisted men, staff.

The 448th had its share of "hot" pilots, but Lt. Locke was not one of them. I appreciated him for that. During all of our months of flying practice missions, the only time he ever did anything that would not have been approved by the C.O. was when, shortly before we finished our training at Sioux City, he buzzed up the Missouri River at tree-top level while we gunners shot at ducks with our fifties. We rationalized it by saying that it was good practice in leading a target. I don't think we hit any but we certainly scattered them.

---

[2] As lead gunner my principal responsibility was to help the others with any problems that occurred with their turrets and equipment.

**Portrait of the author taken on October 1943 while the 448th was stationed at Sioux City Army Air Base, Iowa.**

About the middle of October word came from above that all personnel of the 448th and the 445th, which also was training at Sioux City, were to assemble at the parade grounds, fall into a formation, and march past a reviewing stand. Naturally we did a lot of griping about what we considered a waste of our time, but we assembled, we marched and we were reviewed. After it was all over, as Shorty and I were heading back to our barracks, we saw a very tall, slender captain approaching and prepared to salute him. When we took a second look, we realized that it was Jimmy Stewart, who was the C.O. of one of the 445th's squadrons. We gave him a snappy salute, which he returned. I could hardly wait to write my parents that I had saluted Jimmy Stewart, one of my favorite actors and a contributing factor to my becoming a gunner.

In early November word came that we would be leaving Sioux City in a few days to be processed for overseas duty. At that point the base phone center, where we could place long distance calls, was flooded with men wanting to call home, for no phone calls would be permitted after we left Sioux City. Since at that time a long distance call could take a relatively big bite out of a month's pay, we rarely placed one; in fact, I had never called home, though I wrote at least a short letter every day. Shorty and I decided we had better take advantage of this last opportunity and joined the line of men waiting to call. I talked for nearly an hour to my parents and, as I recall, paid approximately ten dollars, but felt it had been worth every cent. I had already written them that we would soon be heading overseas, so I didn't have to break that piece of news to them.

# CHAPTER 5: ASSIGNED TO THE MIGHTY EIGHTH AIR FORCE

In early November the 448th moved from Sioux City to Herington, Kansas, for final staging and checking out for overseas duty. That Lt. Locke had by this time proven himself to be one of the best was demonstrated when the commanding officer of the 448th, Col. Thompson, selected our crew as the one he would fly with to Herington; thus, we were the last plane to leave Sioux City. It was unfortunate that he did so, for we had no more than got off the ground when I looked out the waist window and saw gasoline streaming out of the right wing filler cap, which had come loose. Using the intercom, I notified Lt. Locke of the problem, and I still remember his response:

"O.K. We're going back in," he calmly responded, just as though it were an everyday occurrence.

We landed without mishap. Uppermost in my mind was the danger of fire, and I was very, very relieved to get back down safely.

Col. Thompson said nothing to anyone but went into the operations office and wrote out an order busting Virgil from tech sergeant to private. Virgil had assigned Pete, our assistant engineer, the responsibility for checking the filler caps during the pre-flight inspection. Thompson did not bother to inquire into why the problem had occurred, but that was his way of doing things. He was not a popular person with the 448th personnel. Part of his problem may have been that he was originally a career infantry officer.

The Colonel said nothing to either Lt. Locke or Virgil about the action he had taken, and we did not get the bad news until two or three days later at Herington. Virgil was understandably furious and insisted he was going to refuse to fly, which he could have done, since flying was voluntary. Nothing that the other enlisted crew members or I said swayed him. Later that evening, however, Lt. Locke came to our quarters and, by assuring Virgil that his tech sergeant rank would be restored soon after our arrival overseas, calmed him down. That promise was kept. An inspection showed that the fuel cap was faulty, so neither Virgil nor Pete was at fault. Unfortunately, Col. Thompson had left and couldn't be told about the faulty cap, but we all doubted that he would have acknowledged that he had made a mistake and rescinded his order taking away Virgil's rank. If he saw Lt. Locke's request to restore Virgil's rank after we arrived at our overseas destination, he did not stop it. It probably had only to be approved by someone at 715th headquarters, so I doubt if it went past him.

**The official patch of the 715th Squadron that appears on the author's jacket in the above photo**

**The author in November 1943 at Herington, Kansas, where 448th crews were checked out for overseas duty.**

At Herington we had our records checked, made out wills, received booster shots, had final medical checkups (my report included a waiver for being underweight for my height), and completed paperwork associated with desired changes in allotments and other matters. Since Dad's working hours left him little time for such things as going to the bank, I filled out a power of attorney form authorizing Mother to take care of my business matters and mailed it home together with my will. In addition to the $144 a month I had been making, I would now receive an additional 20% combat pay. I signed an allotment form to have all but $24 a month sent home. Mother set up an account in my name at a building and loan association, which paid better interest than a bank, and deposited each of my allotment checks of $120 while I was overseas.

The few days we spent at Herington dragged by. The weather was quite disagreeable. In a letter to my parents dated November 7, I wrote: "The more I see of Kansas the less I like it. It rained all day yesterday and turned cold. Now today it's snowing...It isn't snowing very hard but the wind is blowing and it's cold and damp." We made a practice flight or two, but most were cancelled because of the weather. The base itself was a rather drab place, with little in the way of grass or trees. The barracks were as drab as their surroundings. They were "temporaries," buildings erected quickly that were not intended to be used after the war, and provided little more than metal double bunks for sleeping. Since we were restricted to the base and made only a few practice flights, we sat around in the barracks and speculated on what the future held for us. I continued writing my daily letters home, but the lack of activity and the fact that our letters were now being censored left little to write about. We were relieved when, on November 17, our orders to leave finally came through.

**Before beginning their flight to England, the Al Locke crew named their plane *Heaven Can Wait*. This is a copy, much reduced in size, of a painting by Ingemar Melin of Sweden that was done for Melinda Stanley, granddaughter of Locke.**

Our next stop was Morrison Field near West Palm Beach, our point of departure for overseas duty. We had not yet been told where we were to serve; thus, rumors about our destination were the main topic of conversation. The consensus, though, was that we were headed for England in our new B-24H models, the latest series of the Liberator. We had agreed to name ours *Heaven Can Wait* but had not gotten around to having the name painted on our plane. As it developed, we never did.  Lt. Delclisur called his nose turret "Spittin' Kitten," but when I didn't come up quickly with a clever name that I liked, I left it unnamed.

During our flight to Morrison Field Shorty decided to practice operating his ball turret.  As he was lowering the turret, the entrance hatch lid fell off and sailed to the ground.  Since no replacements were available at Morrison Field, one had to be ordered; thus, our departure was delayed and we were one of the last crews to take off for overseas.  In a letter to my parents, I mentioned the loss of the door.  Many years later, on reading some of my letters which Mother had saved, I discovered that the censor had cut out my reference to the lost door.  Why he thought that should be considered confidential information is difficult for me to understand.

The lid finally came, and we took off on November 20 for what we were reasonably certain was England.  Based on our point of departure, however, we could also be headed for Italy or even India.  In the cockpit was a sealed order telling us where we were headed which was not to be opened until we had been airborne for two hours.  Once we had taken off, no crew member could have leaked the information to anyone, so I have no idea why the two-hour delay was mandated. For now, all we knew for certain was that our first stop was Puerto Rico, which we had been told had an excellent PX (post exchange).

Looking out the waist window as the Florida coast faded from view, I wondered how long it would be before I saw the United States again. I even thought about the possibility that I might not return, but as an incurable optimist, I was not worried, although a little apprehensive about what lay ahead.

During the entire flight I sat by the waist window and marveled at the blue of the Caribbean. I had never seen anything like it before. The further south we went, the more intense the blue. Occasionally a small uninhabited island slipped beneath us. As we flew over a huge cumulus cloud, Lt. Locke called on the intercom and said for us to take a look at the cloud. Looking out a waist window at the cloud below, we saw the shadow of our plane in the center of a circular rainbow. That phenomenon is known as a "glory" and appears on the cloud below when it contains ice crystals.

Two hours out, Lt. Locke opened the sealed envelope: we were assigned to the Eighth Air Force in England. After Puerto Rico, our orders called for stops at Trinidad; Belem and Natal, Brazil; Dakar, on the western coast of Africa; Marrakech, French Morocco; then England. Combat might be ahead of us, but the next several days promised to be interesting. Had we gone overseas during the summer, we would have taken the North Atlantic route, a shorter but very humdrum trip compared to the southern route for which we were scheduled.

A few minutes after noon we landed at Puerto Rico and took the line taxi to a large brick building that served as a barracks, where we checked in and were issued our bedding, which included sheets, and assigned to quarters. After making our beds, the other enlisted men and I walked to the PX, which we found to contain a larger assortment of merchandise than any we had seen in the U.S. I suppose the AAF wanted to give its men one last opportunity to purchase anything they might need. The stock included all kinds of clothing, toilet items, knives, watches, books and magazines and, of course, souvenirs, as well as many other items. Since I had loaded up before leaving the States and found no souvenirs that I appealed to me, I purchased nothing other than a few candy bars.

All the clerks were Puerto Rican girls who spoke both Spanish and English. As Pete, Shorty and I stood side by side looking at souvenirs in a case, another clerk approached the one waiting on us and spoke to her in Spanish. Pete grinned and said something back to them in Spanish. The girls looked surprised and a little embarrassed. As we walked away, I asked Pete, "What was that all about?"

He laughed. "The clerk that walked up to the one waiting on us said that the souvenirs were priced much too high, and I asked if we could have a discount." Even though Pete looked very much Mexican, the girls had not anticipated his understanding every word they said.

After the evening meal we went to one of the post theaters. The film was obviously not made in Hollywood, for the photography and acting were considerably below Hollywood standards for even very low budget movies. All of the dialog was in Spanish, with English captions printed at the bottom. Most of the people in the audience were Puerto Rican natives, who applauded and cheered the hero during his first few appearances on the screen.

On returning to our quarters we found several new arrivals who were on their way back to the States after completing their missions with the Eighth Air Force. Naturally, we had lots of questions, for the most part dealing with anti-aircraft fire, enemy fighter opposition, fighter escort for our bombers, and conditions on the bomber bases. The response was not encouraging on the whole. Flak could be very heavy and accurate, enemy fighters were plentiful and effective, and our fighter escort was inadequate, though it had improved recently. They had no official statistics but, based on their own experience, reported that less than half of the crews finished their missions. Shorty and I wondered if they might be exaggerating, but I had the impression that they were not. Still, I was enough of an optimist not to let it worry me—somehow I would come through, I believed.

Since the flight to Trinidad was a short one, we were not scheduled to take off until mid-morning the next day and had lunch before being transported to our plane. Before going to the mess hall, we had checked in the bedding that we had been issued the day before. When my turn came, I saw the clerk credit me with my sheets, even though I had not yet placed them on the counter. I yielded to temptation and walked away with two sheets that went with me to England, where I anticipated being the envy of everyone in my barracks.

On the short flight to Trinidad we were told to look for a life raft, for a plane (not one belonging to the 448th) had gone down two or three days previously. We saw nothing, however.

Because we had to pull a fifty-hour inspection of our plane which kept us busy until bedtime, we saw very little of the field at Trinidad. At dawn the next day we took off for Belem, Brazil, an eight-hour flight.

As on the first two days of flying, we saw nothing but water until mid-morning, when we passed over the coast of South America. Now we found ourselves above a jungle that seemed as vast as the Atlantic that we had just left behind. Since we were flying only a few hundred feet above the jungle, we had a good view. Mile after mile of dark-green treetops passed beneath us, broken only rarely by a small clearing in which there might be a hut or two. Before leaving

Morrison Field, we had been given special parachute harnesses with a backpack holding a machete, simple fishing tackle, first aid kit, compass, and a pack of K-rations. Even in the unlikely event that we were to survive a crash landing in the jungle, I figured that our chances of surviving in that jungle with what we had in the parachute pack were next to none. I would be glad when we left it behind.

At length our course led us back to the coast, which we followed to the mouth of the Amazon River. Even at our cruising speed of about 150 mph, crossing the mouth of the river required several minutes, in the process of which we passed over the equator. Belem was a short distance south of the Amazon.

Because of a minor mechanical problem with the plane, we remained at the Belem air base for two days but were not permitted to go into the city. With little to do on the base, we were relieved when, on the morning of Thanksgiving Day, November 24, we departed for Natal, Brazil, our last stop on this side of the Atlantic. Since this would be another short flight, we did not take off until around 11:00 A.M., so were served an early Thanksgiving Day meal of turkey and all the trimmings before going to our plane. While the food was good, I thought of my parents getting together with the rest of the family around a table loaded with that special home-cooked turkey with oyster dressing, mashed potatoes and gravy, and two or three vegetables, followed by at least two kinds of pie, one of which would be pumpkin. Afterwards, the men would play pinochle or pitch while the women engaged in small talk. How I wished I could be with them!

Since this was one of our shortest flights, we landed at Natal by mid-afternoon. The base here had much better facilities than the one at Belem, such as a larger PX and tents with wood floors rather than the earth floors of the Belem tents. The warm, pleasant nights made sleeping in tents no hardship. Our cots were surrounded by a frame covered with mosquito netting to ward off night insects that would otherwise have been a problem. We were told to check our shoes before putting them on to make sure there were no uninvited guests such as spiders and scorpions. The food at this base was excellent, better than that at most of the U.S. bases where I had been stationed. It was well prepared—no half-done or over-cooked meats or vegetables—and we received ample servings.

Lt. Locke came up with some reason to get the plane grounded so that we could not leave the next morning, which cleared the way to our getting passes into town (engines of Air Forces planes landing at Natal seemed to have a propensity for developing minor problems, for ours wasn't the only that was spending an extra night there). On alighting from the army truck that took us into Natal, we were met by a swarm of natives selling souvenirs. To escape from them we each bought a small trinket and then set out to see the town. Before leaving West Palm Beach, we had been told that numerous Natal stores sold watches, many of them expensive name brands priced at half their cost in the States. The explanation was that prior to December 1941, Germany had given a huge quantity of watches to Brazil in exchange for other products. All were loot taken from occupied countries. I bought a Movado watch for fifty dollars that sold for over one hundred in the U.S.

Natal, which got its name from the word for Nativity, was founded on Christmas Day, 1599. Unfortunately, we were too occupied with shopping to think about taking time for a tour of the historic section of the city. There probably would not have been enough time anyway, for we had to return to camp late that afternoon, November 26, to prepare for an 11:00 P.M. take-off for Dakar, Africa. Departure at that hour would enable the navigator to use celestial navigation for the early part of the flight; also, it would bring us to Dakar in the daylight, when the city and other landmarks could be more easily spotted, thus facilitating a quick landing if fuel happened to be running low, a very real possibility because of the length of the flight. We were the first group to make the flight without auxiliary gas tanks in the bomb bay; thus, accurate navigating was imperative.

As we walked to our plane along a dark street, we saw stacks of boxes of pineapples sitting unguarded outside the mess hall. Two hours later when we took off, the two rear bomb bays contained several dozen pineapples. We also had an extra passenger—John Hortenstine had bought a parrot in Natal, which went to England with him. As it later developed, he did not keep the parrot very long, for a few weeks after our arrival it ate some insignia off his blouse, which resulted in a quick trip into Norwich and the sale of the bird.

At the briefing for our 1,200 mile flight to Dakar, all of which was over water, our officers were warned of the presence of German submarines off the African coast that could duplicate the Dakar radio-range signal and thus lead an aircraft off course. A navigator would have to be sure that his compass reading checked with the radio range. Since Lt. Hortenstine had demonstrated his ability as a navigator during our training flights and on our overseas journey, we were quite confident he would get us there.

This was by far the most monotonous leg of our trip to England, most of which I spent either sitting or sleeping in the waist, for even after daylight came, there was nothing to see but "water, water everywhere." Thus, the appearance of the African coast on the horizon that morning was a welcome sighting. Approximately eleven hours after leaving Natal, we approached Dakar, and those of us in the waist of the plane sat down for the landing. When we touched down, I heard a rumble that startled me. Something had to be wrong with our Lib. On jumping up and looking out the waist window, however, I saw that the landing strip was a steel mat rather than the concrete we were used to.

Regulations required that our plane be fumigated before we could exit—the local officials wanted no South American bugs; Africa had enough of its own. While we waited, Shorty, Hank, Pete, and I sat down in the waist section to eat pineapples. On finishing mine and tossing the core and peelings out the window, I heard a loud commotion and the sound of scuffling. Looking out the window, I saw below me four of the blackest men I had ever seen, fighting over the remainder of my pineapple.

When our gas tanks were checked, not enough gasoline was left to more than dampen the bottom of the measuring stick. Because of unexpected head winds, we had consumed more gas than normal. If Lt. Hortenstine had not hit Dakar right on the nose, we would have ditched in the Atlantic.

Because of bad weather between Dakar and Marrakech, our next destination, we remained at Dakar for several days. The field was just a short distance from the ocean, where the army had reserved an excellent beach for the sole use of its men. We spent most of our time on this beach, swimming and sunning ourselves (I acquired a sunburn worse than the one at gunnery school) and picking up small, colorful shells. After we settled at our base in England, I mailed the shells home. When Mother opened the package, the stench was bad, very bad, for although I had attempted to pull the original occupants from the shells, a residue had remained. She had to spread them outside for several days to eliminate the odor.

An army truck took us to the beach each day on a road winding through a section of the native quarter. I was appalled by the filth of this section and wondered how a human could survive under such conditions. The natives, though, did not seem to mind and grinned from ear to ear at us as we drove by. After each meal, natives came to the mess hall to salvage all they could from the garbage cans. When, as a child, I refused to eat something on my plate, Mother would tell me how a child in such-and-such a country would be glad to have it, and now that truth was driven home most forcefully.

Although transient enlisted personnel were not permitted to go into town (the restriction did not apply to officers), Hank Boisclair was not one to be stopped by what he considered to be petty rules. He found an unguarded place in the fence and made a successful excursion into Dakar. He came back with several native carvings, one of which he sold to me. A head carved from ebony, it supposedly was an idol that had hung on the wall of a native hut. I was quite pleased with my purchase and looked forward to hanging it on the wall of my room back in Quincy.

Finally the weather cooperated, and on December 1 we left for Marrakech, in French Morocco, where we landed shortly before dark. It was cold and damp. I was surprised to find such weather in Africa, which I had always thought of as hot and dry. The contrast with Dakar was a striking one. The tents to which we were assigned had no stoves and were, therefore, cold. Tired from the lengthy flight, we went to bed immediately. Although I had four blankets over me, I awakened during the night so cold that I put on my shirt and trousers and threw my overcoat on top of the blankets. I was still not warm. The problem was that because we had no mattresses for our canvas cots, the cold came in from below. I needed more blankets beneath me.

Storms between Morocco and England delayed our departure, then Cappy, our radio operator, caught the flu and went to the hospital. I immediately commandeered three of his blankets to place on my cot and then kept reasonably warm. Virgil became very sick also and belonged in the hospital as well, though he was never admitted.  Consequently, we remained at the base for eight days, during which we spent most of our time in the city of Marrakech.

A majority of the population were Arabs, many of whom made their living selling souvenirs.  One of our main pastimes was sitting at a table of one of the sidewalk cafes, drinking wine and bargaining with the Arabs for souvenirs.  Most of the time we were not interested in what they were selling, but merely argued with them to see how much we could get them to lower their prices.  One Arab had a hassock cover that I thought Mother would like.  His asking price was $40.00, but after a half-hour's haggling, I paid him $7.00.  Before leaving Marrakech, I also purchased two hand-tooled leather billfolds and two knives, one of which was an old one with a brass sheath.  The other was a small one with a multi-colored glass handle that I thought would make a good letter opener.  I wondered if the Arabs ever washed their long, flowing robes, for few of them looked clean.  They may have been too busy getting rich at the expense of the Americans to bother with washing.

One evening as I came from the Red Cross center after showering, an Arab stopped me and offered to trade souvenirs for the towel I was carrying, one of two extra white ones which I had purchased in Sioux City. When I told him I was not interested, he began offering cash. He really wanted that towel. I do not remember what I finally sold it for, but it was an outlandish price.

The Red Cross center in Marrakech was an excellent one. It was in a beautiful building which housed a theatre, game rooms, reading rooms, lunch room and barber shop. The personnel were most friendly. The latrine facilities at the base were poor; hence, we did all of our showering and shaving at the center. If we were inclined to indulge in a little luxury, we could get a barber shave for a dime. Through the years since the war, I have heard some ex-servicemen complain about the Red Cross, primarily because they were asked to pay for items. My contacts with the Red Cross, on the other hand, were always positive. Before we left for overseas, the Red Cross gave each of us a kit containing cigarettes, candy, stationery, soap, razor blades, a deck of cards, and a few other items. Later in England, I sometimes paid for items from the Red Cross, but the cost was always reasonable. They would have cost me more elsewhere.

If anyone on our crew could have been classified as a character, Hank was the one. In Puerto Rico he had bought a case of rum to take to England, and as mentioned above, he had gone into the off-limit native quarter of Dakar to buy hand-carved items. The day after our arrival in Marrakech, Hank learned that there was an army-supervised house of prostitution nearby and that the army even provided transportation (how's that for "your tax dollars at work"!). He made daily trips and, after the first one, had reservations made for the same Arab lady each day. He took her food and cigarettes each trip. Hank said that his Arab lady was married and worked at this trade with the approval of her husband in order to supplement their income. I suspect she made more than her husband. Hank also decided that he wanted to see what hashish was like and went into an off-limit section of Marrakech to buy some. We feared that he might get a knife in the back, for we had been told of several instances of soldiers being attacked and were warned to wear our sidearms (a .45) into town, which we did. He did come back with some hashish—that is what it was supposed to be, at least. When he smoked the stuff, it had absolutely no effect on him and tasted terrible. It was probably sawdust.

Except for Cappy and Virgil, our radio operator and engineer, we thoroughly enjoyed the week's stay at Marrekech forced on us by Cappy's illness and the inclement weather, since our time was our own except that each of the enlisted men had to take a turn at guarding our plane for one night. The night I took my turn at guarding the plane, I absent-mindedly did something that could have had serious consequences. I was sitting in the radio operator's seat behind the cockpit and, to kill some time, decided to clean and oil my .45. After reassembling the gun, I pointed it straight up above my head, as we had been taught always to do, and pulled the trigger to be sure the gun was working properly. To my horror a loud explosion reverberated throughout the plane. Without thinking what I was doing, I had automatically inserted a clip of ammunition into the .45 before cocking and firing it. I could not even remember picking up the clip. I was reluctant to look up for fear that the bullet had struck something vital; fortunately, it had not. After I pounded the aluminum back in place around the bullet hole in the top of the fuselage, I was relieved to see that the hole could hardly be detected if one did not know it was there. I maintained a discreet silence, and no one ever noticed the place where the bullet had gone through.

After the weather settled down and Cappy and Virgil were healthy enough to return to duty, we prepared to take off for the lengthy flight to England around midnight on December 9. The 448th lost two crews in its exodus to England, both of which came on the Marrakech to England flight. One crew crashed on taking off. The other crew's plane developed an engine problem and, in attempting to return to Marrakech, the crew got lost in the dark and crashed in the Atlas Mountains. All of us, I think, were relieved when we knew we were clear of the mountains. Because it was quite cool and was too dark to see anything below us, we closed the waist windows to shut out the blast of air coming through them. I put on my sheepskin-lined coat and pants and lay down on the floor to try to sleep, but with no success.

Lt. Locke and Lt. Hortenstine were given very specific instructions on the route to take to make sure we cleared the coast of Portugal and Spain and did not over-fly German-occupied France or even get so close to the continent that we might be attacked by enemy fighters. We were supplied with ammunition, and each gunner spent the latter part of the flight at his assigned station. My tail turret had a padded seat, thus was actually more comfortable than sitting on a box or the floor in the waist. After about an hour of scanning the sky for any sign of an enemy fighter, I began to get drowsy from the lack of sleep and the monotony of the flight. To keep from dozing off, I got out of the turret occasionally and stretched my legs and arms for a few seconds before getting back into it. I was quite relieved when Lt. Locke announced over the intercom that land was in sight.

We learned later that one 448th crew had got off course and, thinking they were over England, had attempted to land on the first airfield they saw. The field, however, was not in England but France. According to James Hoseason's account of the incident in *The 1,000 Day Battle*,[3] the Germans used a flare to direct them to a landing strip; however, on their approach the crew saw German markings on parked planes, retracted their landing gear, and began to climb. The German

---

[3] James Hoseason, *The 1,000 Day Battle* (1979: Gillingham Publications), p. 63.

anti-aircraft scored hits on one wing, but the crew made it to England, where they made a forced landing in Wales.

In late afternoon we landed at St. Mawgan airfield, near Newquay on the southwest coast of England. As we waited for a truck to pick us up, snow began falling, and the wind coming off the ocean just a few yards from where our plane was parked was bitterly cold. I was not at all impressed by England at this point and thought it an inauspicious beginning to our stay in this country.

That evening we rode an army truck into Newquay, where we heard our first "Any gum, chum?" request from an English lad. We also had our first experience with blackout. Store fronts were darkened, street lights remained unlit, window shades of homes were pulled down. The only break in the darkness, made more intense by the heavy overcast, was provided by an occasional stab of light from a pedestrian's flashlight or the shaded headlights of a car. None of us had thought to bring a flashlight. How do you find anything in a strange town under these conditions, we wondered. We finally located a pub and entered. When we approached the bar, the barmaid rattled off something to me. I had heard about the English accent, of course, but was not prepared for what I had just heard.

"What?" I asked.

Her second attempt came through no better than the first, and I had to ask for another chance. On the third try I caught enough to realize that she was only asking what I wanted to order. Of all the English people I talked to subsequently, this barmaid was the most difficult to understand. In fact, I had little problem with anyone else. I suppose she thought I was a little dense.

We soon decided that, lacking flashlights and with no experience in getting around in a blackout, we might as well catch the truck taxi back to our quarters and go to bed. Hopefully, England would look better on a sunny day.

# CHAPTER 6: LIFE AT SEETHING

The next morning, December 11, we made the short flight to the 448th base, referred to as Seething, which was the name of a nearby small village about seven miles from Norwich, a city in Norfolk about 100 miles north of London. Because of a low cloud cover, we flew only a few hundred feet above the countryside. I was surprised by how small the hedge-bordered fields were compared with those back home. In spite of the lack of sunshine, I was getting a much better impression of England than I had formed the previous night. Even though it was December, various shades of green predominated, for the light snow of the previous day had disappeared. I liked the neat, ordered appearance of the small fields. On landing at Seething, we were led by someone in a jeep to one of the hardstands, circles of concrete by a taxi strip on which planes were parked. A truck soon arrived and transported us to our quarters. We learned that the majority of the ground personnel had gone from Sioux City to New York, where they boarded the *Queen Elizabeth* on November 23 and arrived at Seething about ten days later.

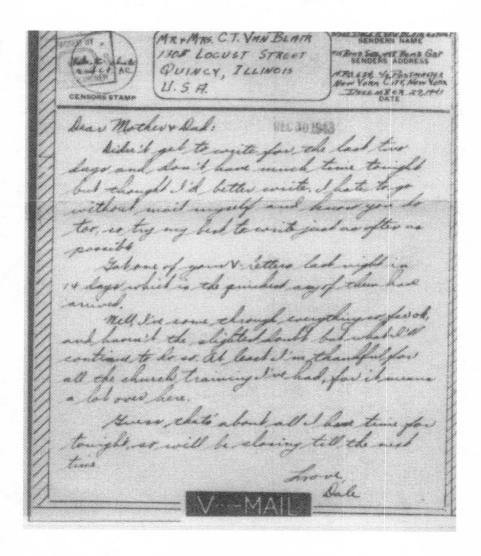

**A V-Mail letter written by the author to his parents. Although the government encouraged the use of V-Mail to save shipping space, the author and most of his friends began using air mail soon after their arrival in England because it was faster and letters were not limited to one rather small page.**

I was very happy to find mail waiting for me, letters from Mother (Dad wrote occasionally, but Mother did most of the writing) and Jane, the girl whom I had met on my furlough and with whom I had corresponded ever since. Since we had not remained any place long enough to receive mail on our flight to England, this was the first for me since we left Harlingen, and it was certainly good for my morale. Mail call was usually the highlight of each day for a G.I., and a man's morale suffered when too many days went by without his receiving a letter from home. Mail delivery from the U.S. to England was good, on the whole, and I rarely went without letters for more than two or three days. Because it would save space in shipping, we were encouraged to use V-Mail (the "V" stood for "victory"), which consisted of a single page on which we were to write our letter. This was then photographed and converted into film, with hundreds of letters stored in one roll. On arrival in the U.S., it was converted back to a letter and delivered to the designated address. Civilians in the U.S. were also encouraged to use V-Mail. One disadvantage was that the user was limited to one page. We soon discovered that we could send a letter of several pages by airmail, which cost only six cents, that would get to its destination more quickly than V-Mail. After the first few weeks all the letters I sent and received went by airmail.

As we sat around that evening talking to others in our hut, they told us about the welcome which the 448th had received from Germany. One of the men had bought a radio on his first trip into Norwich, and since German stations came in quite clearly and often played better popular music than most of the English stations, he had frequently tuned in to them. As the men were listening to a German station on the new radio, they heard the announcer say, "We welcome the 448th Bomb. Group to the ETO. [European Theater of Operations]. We hope you enjoy your stay here, and we look forward to meeting you."

Seething was quite different from the American bases to which we were accustomed. To begin with, there were no rows of barracks—in fact, no barracks. Instead we were housed in Nissen huts, metal half-round structures sometimes called Quonset huts. Because of the necessity of camouflage from German air attacks, the huts were not in neat rows, but rather were placed here and there—under trees, wherever possible. Instead of being heated by forced-air furnaces, each hut had a coke or charcoal stove about thirty inches high and eighteen in diameter, quite small for the space the stove had to heat. The charcoal had to be started with wood, which, in turn, had to be obtained somewhere. Immediately behind our hut was a wooded area from which we could usually scrounge enough dead limbs to start a fire. Since starting a decent one would take from thirty minutes to an hour, we tried not to let the fire go out at night in times when an ample supply of charcoal was available. Our crew was fortunate in that our area in the hut was close to the stove. One disadvantage was that the heat drew men from the other end of the hut, so that our area was often overcrowded.

Although most of the men slept on double metal bunks, there were a few singles, three of which were in the area assigned to our crew, and Shorty and I claimed two of these side by side. The advantage was that one did not get awakened by someone bouncing around in the top bunk, for the double bunks were not all that stable. We were issued six blankets, and it sometimes took all of them to stay warm. Since we had mattresses to stop the cold air from underneath, we could pile all our blankets on top of us. The mattresses, instead of being a single unit, consisted of three pads about two feet square placed inside a mattress cover and were commonly referred to as "biscuits." They were not too comfortable and tended to separate, leaving a gap of two or three inches. When I made up my bed that first night, I caused quite a stir when I nonchalantly produced my two sheets that I had "borrowed" on checking out at my Puerto Rico barracks. During my year in England, I knew no one else with sheets, for they were very scarce in the stores, and the 8th Air Force did not furnish them.

All in all, the huts were quite drab—as I heard it described once, a man-made cave. Blackout curtains covered the windows, and two or three overhead light bulbs struggled to illuminate the hut. A small shelf served to hold each man's personal possessions such as photos. Contrary to the impression given by some Hollywood movies, the walls were not plastered with pictures of pin-up girls. Only a few men in my hut had them. A foot locker held each man's clothing. No tables or chairs were provided, so when I wrote a letter, I put something firm on my knees and used that as a writing platform. My cot was both my bed and my chair. Those with upper bunks either had to sit with their legs dangling down or sit on the bed of someone willing to share space. The occasional poker game took place on one of the participant's beds. The enlisted men of either four or five crews (24-30 men) were housed in our hut. During the three months that I flew with the 448th, only two crews were lost from our hut, substantially better than average.

**The 448th control tower, which now is a museum honoring the men of the group. The author took this photo on a trip to England in 1986.**

Seething was a newly constructed field, and it showed. Mud was everywhere, including walks and roads. The difference between the walks and the unpaved areas was that the walks provided a firm bottom for the mud. We tracked mud into our huts, the mess hall, and every other building we entered. One good thing I can say about Col. Thompson, our C.O., is that he did not order any quarters inspections during those first few weeks. The day after arriving at Seething, Shorty and I went to Supply to get overshoes. By the time we arrived at Supply, our shoes were so muddy that we couldn't put on the overshoes for the return trip because we would have had difficulty getting the inside of the overshoes cleaned out.

Showering and shaving was a sporadic affair. Central showers were available, but hot water usually was not. As I recall, we might have averaged hot water one day of every seven to ten, and then for only two or three hours before the supply ran cold (nothing like getting all soaped up and then having the hot water run out). Someone from our hut would come in with the news that the water was hot, and there would then be an exodus to the shower room. As for shaving, no one did it regularly. I probably averaged shaving every three days. Since hot water usually was not available and eliminating a three-day growth with cold water was—for me, at least—a painful experience, I would fill my steel helmet with cold water and heat it by dipping a hot stove lid into it. Not liking to wear an oxygen mask for several hours over beard stubble, I always shaved the evening before we were to fly a mission.

Inspections were a rarity. At Seething, however, because of the mud, we swept out the hut regularly and even mopped occasionally. After our crew's subsequent transfer to Hethel, the 389th base, in March, we found mud no longer a problem, since it was an older base than Seething; hence, mopping here was done far less often than at Seething. At Hethel we were permitted to shower on Tuesday and Saturday, but hot water was sometimes not available on those days.

The food at Seething wasn't great but was usually edible. Some complained about the frequency with which spam and tuna on toast (the men had a less dignified name for the latter item: "s—on a shingle") were served, but I didn't mind either. I did not care much for the powdered eggs usually served for breakfast but ate them. One dish that was frequently served which I actively disliked was Brussels sprouts. After the first time or two, I usually passed them by. I still don't care much for them.

Flying personnel had no assigned duties except to fly their missions. Because of the frequency with which bad weather during the winter caused canceled missions, plus the fact that not every crew flew every mission made by the group, we averaged only about a mission a week during the winter months. For example, my eighteen missions spanned seventeen weeks. That left a lot of free time. Poker was a popular pastime with most of the men (I did not participate for several months), and lots of letters were written. Since I wrote my parents at least every three days and frequently more often (I had written every day while in the States) and also corresponded with several other relatives and friends, letter writing occupied quite a bit of my time. We made trips to the Aeroclub, the enlisted men's club, where books and newspapers were available. Movies were shown during the evening at the base theater, and a U.S.O. group occasionally came around to entertain us. Also, we were free to take the truck taxi into Norwich as frequently as we wished. Special passes were required only for overnight or longer leaves.

About a week after settling in at Seething, Cappy, Virgil, Pete, Shorty and I made the first of many trips into Norwich (pronounced

Nor'ich), a city that now has a population of approximately 120,000, so probably ran something less than 100,000 during the war. We took the truck taxi in right after lunch, thus had a few hours of daylight in which to explore. As one who had always had a keen interest in history, I found the city with its narrow, winding streets, some with centuries-old cobblestones, to be a fascinating place. As we wandered around, not really knowing where we were going, we came to Elm Hill, which became one of my favorite places to visit. The narrow, cobbled street was lined with houses, some with shops on the ground level, most of which were at least three hundred years old. At the open-air market, where multi-colored awnings protected the shops and shoppers, I was surprised to see fresh meat hanging out in the open. Even though it was winter, I didn't think I would want to eat beef or pork that had not been stored in a protected and refrigerated case. We explored the eleventh-century Norman castle ruins and then went to Norwich Cathedral, which was founded in 1069. On entering the cathedral, I was not prepared for what I saw. In contrast with the drab gray stone exterior, a huge, long arch of gleaming white marble with Norman columns lay before me. Above the door through which we had entered was a large stained glass window. I had never seen anything like it. The tapered spire, which is 315 feet tall, is the second highest in England. On learning that the Red Cross center was located in the basement of the cathedral, we went there for a cup of tea. Since it was now getting dark and we had been told that the supply of warm English beer was rationed daily and did not last long after the pubs opened their doors each evening, we decided we had better head for the closest pub. On the way I bought my first fish and chips wrapped in newspaper and was surprised to find that the chips were not like our potato chips, but rather were like our French fries. We waited for only a few minutes before the pub opened, and we each managed to get two mugs down before the supply ran out. After watching a game of darts for a few minutes, we caught the truck back to our base.

On December 22 the 448th made its first mission, but we were not alerted to fly. Twenty-six crews took off for Osnabruck, Germany, a manufacturing center. Only thirteen made the mission; the others returned early because of not being able to get into formation as a result of bad weather and lack of experience. The thirteen making the mission were attacked at the German border by ME-109s and FW-190s (ME is the abbreviation for Messerschmitt; FW, for Focke Wulf) with a loss of three aircraft (thirty men) and five others heavily damaged. The returnees we had talked to in Puerto Rico had apparently not been exaggerating. The crew whose beds were next to ours went on the mission and came back eager to tell us what it was like. Their tales of the flak and the German fighter attacks were hardly reassuring. Because of their inexperience, the pilots failed to maintain a close formation so that the gunners could direct a concentrated fire at the attacking fighters. The Germans were thus able to fly through the formation to attack our bombers without too much danger of being shot down themselves. To make matters worse, photographs of the target taken two days later showed no damage done. It was not an auspicious beginning, but it was a good day for us to have remained on the ground.

Not all of the hazardous flying was done over enemy territory. Take-offs and assembling into formation sometimes resulted in crack-ups and collisions. Because our bombers were frequently overloaded, they could take almost every foot of runway before lifting off.

Occasionally one would not make it and run off the end. If luck rode with the crew, the men escaped with nothing but a damaged plane; if not, lives were lost. What crews dreaded even more than taking off was the overcast that prevailed more often than not, which made it impossible to see nearby planes. In such a case, the pilot had to use his instruments (altimeter, air speed indicator, etc.) to follow a prescribed course, speed, and rate of climb, and any deviation was hazardous. Near misses were common, and collisions occurred which resulted in the loss of two planes and twenty lives. I no longer remember on which mission it happened, but on one occasion we narrowly missed colliding with another plane that was off the prescribed course.

On the evening of December 23, we were alerted to fly our first mission the next day, Christmas Eve day. All the crews in our hut were to fly, so since the orderly would come to awaken us at 3:30 A.M., we all went to bed early. One of the men on the crew that had gone on the December 22 mission called out, "Say your prayers, boys!" I did, but in view of the scant attention I had given Him since entering service, I don't know why I thought He would listen.

Although I thought I might have trouble going to sleep, I did not. The next thing I knew the orderly was there to turn on the lights and call out, "Time to get up!" I put on a pair of long underwear, then a wool shirt and a pair of wool trousers. I pulled on three pairs of socks, two light ones and a pair of heavy wool ones. Next came a heavy wool sweater. I wore my leather flight jacket to breakfast but would replace it with the sheepskin-lined one at the plane.

The pre-mission routine was always the same. We would be awakened early, usually about 3:30 A.M., quickly dress, and go to the mess hall for a big breakfast that included fried eggs, the only time we were treated to them (occasionally Shorty and I would get up early when a mission was scheduled for which we were not alerted just to get the combat crew breakfast). From there we went to the briefing rooms, the officers to one and enlisted men to another. The officers received special briefings depending on their responsibilities: the target, formation positions, assembly details, color and radio codes, weather en route to target, likely weather at base at return, etc. Aerial photographs of the target and target area were shown. Navigators received the necessary maps and charts, and bombardiers were given information pertinent to finding the aiming point. When the enlisted men went into their briefing room, a sheet that was taken off to display the target when the briefing began covered a large map of Europe on the front wall. We then would be given some of the same information that was being given to the officers, with special attention to the type of aircraft likely to be encountered and where. Following briefing, we checked out chest parachute packs and electrically heated suits and checked in any personal effects that we did not wish to take with us. Trucks then transported us to the hardstands where our planes were parked. I checked out my tail turret, put on the heated suit and plugged it in to make sure it was working properly, and put on my fleece-lined flying suit over it. I then slipped into the Mae West life preserver and buckled the straps, and on top of that went my parachute harness to which the chest chute could be buckled. After all that, I didn't walk, I waddled about like a duck. I also placed a flak vest and helmet by the tail turret, which I did not put on until just before entering the turret after take-off. It was then a matter of waiting for the time to come to taxi out to the main runway.

The flak vest was made of overlapping steel platelets inside a cloth cover and was intended to protect the vital parts of the upper body. A large majority of wounds suffered by bomber crew members were from fragments from exploding anti-aircraft shells, and the flak vest and helmet provided very effective protection against those fragments. The vest was, I suppose, a precursor to today's bullet-proof vest.

Another vital piece of equipment was the oxygen mask. The B-24 had a demand-type oxygen system—i.e. it automatically adjusted the oxygen flow to the altitude at which the plane was flying. The regulator at each station on the plane had an on-off valve that provided for a flow of pure oxygen if it should be required. If, for example, a man passed out from anoxia (lack of oxygen to the brain), another crew member could administer pure oxygen to help the victim to recover quickly. At 20,000 to 25,000 feet, the altitudes at which we flew our missions, anoxia was an ever-present danger; just a few minutes of it could be fatal. If a crew member had to leave his station for some reason, even if just for a minute or so, it was essential that he use a walk-around oxygen bottle. Because breath condensation could freeze and block the oxygen supply, I made it a practice to check my mask and tube periodically and dislodge any ice that had formed, for anoxia could creep up on a person without his realizing what was happening. I disliked wearing the oxygen mask, for the snug fit caused it to become uncomfortable. The longer the mission, the more uncomfortable it became; however, it performed one useful function besides supplying oxygen: it provided some protection for the face from the blast of frigid air that came in through the open waist windows and back to the tail turret. I was thankful for the fleece collar that could be turned up to keep the cold air from going down the back of my neck.

**A B-24H Liberator. The author flew all his missions in the H model.**

**Exterior view of a B-24 tail turret, in which the author sat on his crew's missions**

Interior view of the tail turret with its back doors open.

The target for our first mission was rocket-launching installations at Labroye in the Pas de Calais area on the French coast. Because No-Ball was the code name given to these sites, we referred to all missions to the launching sites as No-Ball missions. Our plane, *Heaven Can Wait*, was loaded with 500-pound general-purpose bombs and ten rather nervous crew members. I was concerned about how I would react to being shot at, whether by flak (anti-aircraft fire) or an enemy fighter. I thought I could remain calm but could not be sure until it happened.

The 448th put up twenty-seven Libs to fly in formation with the 93rd and 446th. When our turn came to take off, Lt. Locke revved up the engines and released the brakes, and our plane lumbered down the runway. With a 5000-pound bomb load, our plane didn't pick up speed quite as rapidly as we were used to, but I felt it lift off well before the end of the runway. After we had gained a few thousand feet of altitude, I got into my tail turret.

Looking around, I could see planes flying every which direction with no apparent pattern prevailing. There was, however, for in due time order emerged from apparent chaos, the pilots nursed their planes into their proper places in the formation, and we crossed the English Channel. As he did on each of our subsequent missions, once we were out of sight of the English coast, Lt. Locke announced over the intercom that gunners should test their guns, and each of us fired a short burst. As we entered French airspace, I saw black puffs of smoke floating past, mostly below us, and realized with some apprehension that we were encountering our first flak. So far the Germans did not have us zeroed in, and I hoped they got no closer with their fire. We soon left that flak behind and were in the clear.

Expecting to see German fighters at any moment, I kept swiveling my head from side to side, but none appeared. As we began the bomb run, we ran into heavy and sustained flak that was coming a little too close for my peace of mind, but I felt nothing more than an anxious desire to complete the bomb run and get out of there. Then I heard Lt. Delclisur's voice over the intercom: "Bombs away!" The formation made a gradual turn away from the target, and we finally moved away from the flak. I took a quick look behind me at Pete and Hank standing by their guns at the waist windows. Pete saw me look back and waved, so I knew everything within his view was all right. I maintained a vigilant lookout for enemy fighters and was most happy when we left the French coast behind without my seeing any. In contrast with the December 22 mission, this one went well, and the

448th lost no planes to enemy action. It was what we termed a "milk run." When we returned to our base, a low ceiling necessitated an instrument let-down, that is, Lt. Locke had to depend almost solely on his instruments rather than sight in descending through the clouds. I found the descent through the clouds to be a little nerve wracking, but everything went well, and Lt. Locke brought *Heaven Can Wait* in for a smooth landing. Three aircraft, however, were heavily damaged in landing mishaps. Our crew now had mission number one behind us; all we had to do was to survive twenty-four more.

Every mission was followed by a debriefing at which we first received a shot of scotch, which was intended, I expect, not only to calm our nerves but also to loosen our tongues. Neither Lt. Locke nor Lt. Delclisur drank, so they gave theirs to other crew members. We then were questioned about the mission. Did we see any of our planes go down? If so, when? Any parachutes seen? What kind of enemy aircraft was encountered? What time? How long did the encounter last? How was the flak? Could you see the bombs hit? If so, where did they strike? And so it went.

On returning to my hut after the debriefing, there on my bed were Christmas packages from Mother and Dad and other family members—every package I had coming was delivered that day. Among them was one from Jane in which was her photograph. I was pleased to be no longer among the few men who did not have a girl friend's photo on his shelf. Not everyone got packages that day, so I assumed that the timely arrival was a fortunate coincidence. At any rate, it made my day.

On Christmas the 448th stood down (did not fly a mission). Although it wasn't the same as home cooking, our Christmas dinner was nevertheless very good, with ample servings of turkey. We spent most of the afternoon at the Aero Club, the enlisted men's club, listening to records and visiting with friends. It certainly beat being involved in the ground war that was going on in the Pacific. It might be cold at 20,000 feet, and we might have to fly through flak and undergo fighter attacks, but from what I had read about jungle warfare, I preferred to go to war in the tail end of a B-24.

# CHAPTER 7: EARNING THE AIR MEDAL

**Billowing clouds provide a backdrop for 448th planes in their way to Germany. Clouds such as these frequently prevailed over England, and taking off into such an overcast was a hazardous undertaking**

**The 448th sets out on one of its early missions.**

On December 30 we made our second mission in *Heaven Can Wait*. To our target, a rubber factory in Ludwigshafen, Germany, we carried forty 100-pound incendiaries. As we anticipated, with the target located in Germany, this was no milk run. The headline in the next day's newspaper read, "2,000 planes in greatest bombing attacks of war," which included about 600 fighters; but in spite of the fighter escort, we were attacked by ME-109s, easily recognized by their long, thin fuselage and large propeller spinners which blended in with the curve of the front fuselage. Each time a German fighter came within view, I used the intercom to call the other crew members and alert them to its location: "109 at seven o'clock high [or wherever it was located]." Each time I saw an enemy plane heading in our general direction, I began tracking it with my gun sight, but none attacked us, which was quite all right with me.

The plane flying on our right wing, piloted by Lt. Tom Foster, was shot down. I did not see it happen because his plane was outside of my range of vision, but other crew members did. An ME-109 came in from the front, firing as it came, and Lt. Foster's plane nosed over and went straight down. Only two of his crew were seen to bail out. The enlisted men were assigned to my Nissen hut and were my friends. Loss of a plane flying next to ours caused me to reflect on the role that luck was going to play in our completing the required twenty-five missions. My optimism was being tested. Two other 448th planes were also lost. As on our first mission, the three groups comprising the 20th Combat Wing (93rd, 446th, and 448th) combined for this strike. This was the last mission we made in *Heaven Can Wait*, for Lt. L. P. Slater and crew took it on a mission the next day to bomb Cognac/Chateaubernard, France, and belly landed it at Yeoveltin, England. Our plane had to be salvaged for parts.

Two 715<sup>th</sup> Squadron, 448<sup>th</sup> B.G., Liberators on an early mission. In the foreground is *Bag o'Bolts,* which the Locke crew flew on its mission of January 4, 1943. The date this photo was taken is unknown.

For the first time after a mission, we returned to our hut and had to look at six empty beds. Instead of the buzz of conversation and joking that followed the mission on December 24, when no planes were lost, there was only some quiet talk, most of it centered around our six friends who had gone down. How often, I wondered, might this be repeated.

January 1, 1944, brought a change in command for the Eighth Air Force. Lt. Gen. James Doolittle, remembered by most Americans as the leader of the B-25s that had bombed Tokyo on April 18, 1942, replaced Gen. Eaker as its commander, with the latter assuming command of the Allied air forces in the Mediterranean. Gen. Spaatz took over command of U.S. Strategic Air Forces in Europe, which meant that he had overall operational command of the 15th Air Force in Italy and the 8th in England. The most immediate effect on bomber crews was the policy regarding fighter escort. Under General Eaker the fighters were expected to stay close to the bombers so that they could quickly respond to attacks by the Germans. General Doolittle almost immediately changed that policy and freed the fighters to range ahead and intercept the Germans wherever they could be found. For obvious reasons, we didn't like Doolittle's decision to free the fighters from close escort, for it was comforting to see the American fighters close by, ready to come to our assistance. The fighter pilots, on the other hand, welcomed the new policy, for it freed them to seek out the Germans and destroy them wherever they could be found. As it developed, however, fighter support was usually not too far away.

Doolittle issued another edict in January that was a blow to the morale of combat personnel: he raised the required number of missions from twenty-five to thirty. It had already become obvious that our chances of completing twenty-five were not too good. How many of us would be lucky enough to do a thirty-mission tour?

The new year brought still another edict that was not quite so drastic: we were to take vitamin pills and cod liver oil capsules, which we received daily, as I recall. Apparently the powers that be were concerned about how we might react to the miserable English weather that we were to experience. Had the cod liver oil not been in tasteless capsules I might have rebelled. I had hated the liquid form as a child and didn't think I would like it any better as an adult.

The weather throughout January was abominable, with numerous missions scrubbed because of bad weather. On several occasions we were alerted, got up in the early morning, went through briefing, made the trip to our plane and waited for take-off time, only to have the mission cancelled. I had mixed feelings about those cancellations. On the one hand, once I had been rousted out of bed early and gone through all the preliminaries, I would have liked to put another mission behind me. After all, I had to complete thirty. On the other hand, I was always a little relieved at not having to risk my life that day, for I found myself thinking that perhaps this would have been the mission on which we would have been shot down.

Because of the sustained bad weather, we made only three missions in January. The first was on January 4, for which we were assigned *Bag o' Bolts*. Because of the length of this one—the target was Kiel, Germany—we were at the hardstand where our plane was parked before dawn. It was pitch black. As I walked around the hardstand, I took one step too far and felt water go over the top of my heavy flying boot. I had stepped into a water-filled hole by the edge of the concrete. Lt. Locke heard of my mishap and came to me to express concern about the possibility of frostbite if I went on the mission. He agreed with me that there might not be enough time left before we were to taxi for take-off to go back for a dry sock and electrically heated shoe and that it might take even longer to have someone from headquarters get a replacement gunner. Besides, I didn't want my crew to go without me. I knew there was danger of frostbite, perhaps a bad case of it, but I was not going to be left behind. Using rags found in the plane, I dried my foot, wrung the water out of the wool sock, and put it back on. I thought it might be best not to wear the two thin socks that I usually wore beneath the wool one on the theory that wet wool next to my skin was better than wet cotton. I plugged in my heated suit and hoped the heated shoe would have time to dry my sock and the inside of my flying boot before we reached an altitude where the temperature got too low for the heated shoe to compensate for any moisture that remained.

We took off, found our place in the formation, and headed across the North Sea, slowly gaining altitude until we reached 23,000 feet. My heated suit and boots were working, but my foot was cold. I would be glad when this mission was over. Some time later I realized that I was getting cold all over—my heated suit was no longer working. The threat of my foot getting severely frostbitten was now a major concern. Then I discovered that the turret did not respond when I moved the control grip and the intercom was out. We were without electric power, which meant that all four generators (each engine had one) had gone out. The situation was, in my view, critical. While turrets could be converted to hand cranks, it was not an effective method of operation and would seriously handicap us if we were attacked by German fighters. I was thankful that the skies remained empty except for the few B-24s behind us.

I was miserably cold, especially my foot. Then I suddenly realized that no other Libs were in sight: we had dropped out of the formation, and the pressure in my ears told me that we were slowly descending. I was relieved that we were going down but concerned about the possibility of enemy fighters catching us with limited firepower away from the formation. Fortunately, none appeared, and before long I began to warm up little by little as we descended to a few hundred feet above the North Sea. The wet foot, however, was very cold. The sea was rough with white-capped waves. This would not be a good day to have to ditch, I thought, and hoped that whatever mechanical problems we had would not prevent our reaching England.

Finally I saw the English coast pass beneath us. We were safe. After landing and parking the plane, Lt. Locke said that he had aborted forty miles from the target because of power failure, a problem with an engine, and a shortage of oxygen. The thermometer needle in the cockpit had hit the peg at sixty below zero, so it was actually colder than that. I had a mild case of frostbite of the toes of my right foot but suffered no long-lasting effects. Had we not aborted, though, my flying days would have been over, for continuing with the formation would have meant more hours of exposure to the extreme sub-zero temperature. Because we had not aborted until we were not far from Kiel, we were given credit for the mission.

After the other crews returned, we learned that as a result of a mix-up over Kiel, a formation of B-17s had released its bombs as it flew over the 448th. Bombs fell on all sides of our planes, narrowly missing some but luckily hitting none. I was glad that we had at least missed that experience. Perhaps if we had been able to continue with the formation, one of those bombs might have struck us.

The next day the 448th returned to Kiel, but we were not alerted. The plane in which Major Squyres, the C.O of our squadron, the 715th, was flying took a direct flak hit in the waist and broke in two. There were no survivors. Major Jack Edwards was appointed our new C.O. The 448th was not faring too well. In its first six missions, sixteen planes had been lost to enemy action, and others had been lost or damaged in landing mishaps. It seemed obvious that more training was required, and pilots spent the next few days practicing formation flying.[4] Gunners were told that, rather than waiting for the enemy to come within range, they should begin firing when a German came reasonably close in an attempt to discourage him from attacking.

One week later, on January 11, we went out again, this time to Meppen, an armament town near Brunswick, carrying ten 500-pound demolition bombs in a plane named *Down and Go.* Although hundreds of German fighters attacked other formations, we saw none and ran into only moderate flak. Over 700 American heavy bombers

---

[4] Hoseason, pp. 72-73, 252.

and 500 fighters hit targets in Germany. Next morning's newspaper reported that sixty bombers were lost, meaning that 600 men were either killed or captured.

I did not know until after we returned that we had been unable to make connections with our own group and had gone over with the 389th, the group to which we would later be transferred.

In a letter that I wrote to my mother and dad that evening, I mentioned that I had begun to do something that I had never done before: read the Bible through from cover to cover. Unfortunately, I did not complete the project; even more unfortunately, I did a rather bad job of applying what I did read.

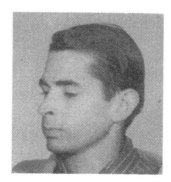

**The author's "escape" photo. Shortly after the 448th arrived at its base at Seething, photos were taken of all flying personnel dressed in civilian clothes. They were intended for use on forged documents in case a downed crew member was lucky enough to be rescued by the French underground. The Germans, unfortunately, were usually able to recognize them.**

We made our last January mission, the fifth over all, on January 29, again carrying 500-pound demolitions, this time to Frankfurt in central Germany.  Our plane was *Vadie Raye*, which we also flew on our next three missions.  There had been a light, wet snow during the night, which the ground crew had cleaned off our plane.  However, on checking my tail turret, I found that some snow remained on the plexiglass and obscured the vision somewhat.  I picked up a rag and walked through the bomb bay to the forward section, climbed through the top escape hatch, and prepared to walk on top of the fuselage back to my tail turret.  The horizon had just barely begun to lighten up a bit, and in the darkness I felt as if I were a hundred feet from the ground instead of about eighteen.  After a few feet, my forward foot slipped a little on a patch of ice, but I carefully stepped over it and had no further problem making it to the turret.  After cleaning it off, I started back.  I had taken only a step or two before my foot slipped just a little on another patch of ice, and suddenly I had the feeling I was going to fall.  I was scared.  A fall from the top of the fuselage to the hardstand was sure to result in serious injury, possibly death.  I

142

stood there a moment, then dropped to my hands and knees and carefully and ever so slowly crawled the approximately sixty feet back to the escape hatch. Along the way I encountered several other patches of ice that were not quite in the center of the fuselage where I had walked going back to the turret. I felt fortunate still to be on top of the plane. After reaching the escape hatch and lowering myself onto the flight deck, I resolved never again to walk the fuselage in the dark.

Finally we saw the green flare shoot up from the control tower, signaling that it was time to taxi out to the main runway. When our turn came to take off at about 8:15, we roared down the runway. When we reached the point where I knew we usually lifted off, we were still earthbound. I was afraid we were not going to make it. Then I felt the landing gear clear the runway just as I saw the end of the runway disappear beneath the open escape hatch through which I was looking. Though there had not seemed to be much ice on the plane, the added weight of what there was had been enough to jeopardize our takeoff.

I had already had enough excitement for one day, and we had not even left England. Fortunately the rest of the mission went well. Our formation was attacked by a few fighters, but our escort quickly drove them off. Before the Germans left, however, I fired my first rounds at an enemy plane, an ME-109. It was out of effective range, but we had been told to try to discourage the Germans from attacking. If I hit him, I did little damage, for he went merrily on his way, but at least he stayed away from us. I watched a twin-engine ME-110, the only one of this type that I saw on any of my missions, at six o'clock low begin a pass at a Lib below us and prepared to fire at him, although he was also out of range. Then I saw a P-38 zoom in on his tail and send him spinning down. If it hadn't been for my oxygen mask, I would have shouted my approval. It was the first German plane I had seen destroyed by one of our fighters. Because of a 10/10 undercast,[5] we dropped our bombs on PFF flares at 21,000 feet. A PFF plane was one equipped with radar that enabled the bombardier to pick out the target through a cloud cover. Although we flew through intense flak over the target, we returned to our base without a single loss. We

---

[5] A cloud cover over the target was rated on a scale of 0-10. A 10/10 undercast

landed a little before 5:00, so were in the air almost nine hours. At the debriefing, I told of seeing the P-38 down the Me-110, and our debriefing officer said he would file a report. Eyewitness evidence such as mine could make the difference in crediting a pilot with a victory.

It was the custom for a crew returning from its fifth mission, which won the Air Medal for each crew member, to buzz the runway; even our go-by-the-book Col. Thompson accepted this breach of regulations. Though Lt. Locke was not a show-off, he followed the accepted procedure. As he roared down the runway not more than a dozen feet above it, an English farmer who lived nearby was walking alongside the runway with a load of kindling on his back. On hearing the noise, he looked behind him, saw us roaring toward him, and dove to the ground. Kindling flew in all directions. We thought it was hilarious, but I expect the farmer was, at the very least, upset, both figuratively and literally.

---

meant that the target was completely covered by clouds.

# CHAPTER 8: A SEVERED HYDRAULIC LINE

On February 1 our crew received a 72-hour pass into London, about one hundred miles south of Norwich. Virgil, Pete, Shorty, and I (Hank and Cappy each elected to go solo) caught the train out of Norwich to London, about a four-hour trip because of the numerous stops made along the way. The coaches, considerably smaller than those in the U.S., consisted of individual compartments with seats facing each other and doors opening directly onto the loading platform; in other words, there was no aisle going the length of the coach and no way to go from one compartment to the adjoining one— also, no access to a rest room!

In London we took a taxi to the Piccadilly Circus area and began looking for a hotel room, but at each hotel we got the same response: no vacancy. Hoping we could find a room if we got away from the Circus, we began walking. It was now dark, and we knew nothing, of course, about London. One thing I did know: I did not want to spend the night walking the streets of London. Then, as we went down a side street, we saw a "Rooms for Rent" sign and knocked at the door to inquire. It was a home owned by a couple who furnished board and room for long-term renters, but since they had four empty beds in a large room, they agreed to put us up for two nights. Somehow the place reminded me of something out of a Horatio Alger, Jr. novel, many of which I had read when I was in grade school, for the inmates looked as if they belonged to the same time period, the early 1900s.

After getting settled, we hurried to the Palace Theatre and arrived in time to see a stage production, a musical comedy entitled "Something in the Air." As an all-English production, it included no songs familiar to us but provided an enjoyable evening. I had never heard of the stars, Jack Hulbert and Cicely Courtneidge, but I suspect they were well known to Londoners, for the musical had been running for several weeks, and the theater was full. Unlike our theaters, waitresses circulated through the audience during the intermission, serving refreshments and taking orders for drinks. We liked that.

The next morning we ate breakfast with our hosts, since it was included with our night's lodging. About a dozen other renters and we all ate together at an extra-long table. I still had the feeling of the early twentieth century, for the men wore stiff white collars and black business suits.

We spent all day Saturday taking in as many of the landmarks as possible, most of which were included on an American-Red-Cross-sponsored taxi tour that cost six shillings, the equivalent of only $1.20 in American money. We drove by or made brief stops in front of 20-25 famous sites, including Buckingham Palace, Houses of Parliament, 10 Downing Street (Prime Minister Winston Churchill's residence), Tower of London, St. Paul's Cathedral and Westminster Abbey. We were given time to make brief tours of only the last two, but what can you expect for $1.20? Of all the places we visited, Westminster Abbey impressed me the most. As I walked around and read inscriptions on blocks of stone in the floor and walls, many of which marked the graves of people about whom I had studied in high school history and literature courses, I thought about what a different perspective Americans have on age compared to that of the English— what was old in the U.S. was almost recent history in England.

That evening we ate at Rainbow Center, the American Red Cross Center at Piccadilly Circus. London, of course, was blacked out, but this time we were prepared with our flashlights. We wandered around the area for a few minutes, in the course of which we were accosted twice by the notorious Piccadilly Commandos, the prostitutes who frequented the area. We said thanks, but no, thanks, and entered the next pub that we saw. We hoped we might be able to meet some English girls, but it didn't work out. About 10:00 P.M., we took a taxi back to our rooming house. Sunday morning after breakfast, we caught our train back to Norwich, where we spent the afternoon before reporting back to base.

Although all gunners had been trained to maintain their guns, ground personnel had been performing that task. Around the first of February, however, an order was issued that gunners would now clean, maintain and reinstall their own guns. Even though it required taking away from my free time, I felt that I would prefer to be responsible for the proper functioning of the guns on which our lives might depend rather than depend on someone else. Also, we probably had more time than the ground crew to perform that task. I never did hear what motivated the order, but it may have been the time factor.

On February 5 we bombed the airport at Tours, France, an uneventful mission with light flak and excellent fighter support. A few FW-190s made one pass at our formation but did little damage and were quickly driven off by our fighters. On February 10 we took off to bomb an airfield in Holland but had to abort before leaving England because of excessive fuel consumption.

Our next mission on February 13, however, did not go as well as the one on February 5. We returned to the Pas de Calais area, the target for our first mission, carrying incendiaries. Contrary to our expectations, this was no milk run like the first. Though I saw no enemy fighters, the flak was extremely heavy and accurate. We had run into quite a bit of flak on our December 24th mission to bomb the rocket-launching sites, but it was much worse this time. The Germans must have moved in more anti-aircraft batteries. After depositing our bombs on the target below, we turned and left the flak behind.

A few minutes after I had left my turret and gone back to the waist as we approached Seething, Lt. Locke sent Lt. Delclisur to tell us that we had problems. Our plane's hydraulic system had been knocked out by a piece of flak that severed a line. Virgil could lower the landing flaps and landing gear manually, but the main concern was that we might have no brakes for the landing. On returning to Seething, we circled the field and fired a flare signaling for an emergency landing, which gave us priority over other planes and brought out the ambulances and fire trucks. Lt. Locke hoped enough fluid was left in the lines for one application of the brakes but could not be sure. As soon as the main landing gear touched down, he dropped the tail so that the skid would drag on the runway and slow the plane down in the hope that when the plane came to the end of the runway, it would be slowed down enough that one application of the brakes would stop it. If the brakes did not work, the plane would hit the mud at the end of the runway, probably tearing off the landing gear but hopefully skidding to a stop with no injuries to the crew. Hank, Pete, Shorty and I went to the back of the tail section so that our weight would put additional pressure on the skid. We barreled down the runway with sparks from the skid streaming behind us. I held my breath as we neared the end of the runway; then felt the plane abruptly slow down as the brakes were applied. The plane lost sufficient speed by the runway's end that Lt. Locke was able to turn onto the taxi strip to clear the runway for other planes. I admired the way he had handled the plane and congratulated him as we stood around talking after exiting the plane. "Well," he laughed, "I'd had enough practice in dragging the skid," referring, of course, to the landing problems he had encountered at Wendover.

We counted fifty-two flak holes in our plane, including two in my tail turret, but no one was injured. We were very fortunate. In spite of the intense flak, the 448th lost no planes, and only four heavy bombers were lost by the Eighth Air Forces, far fewer than most days' losses.

It was becoming clear to me that because of my isolated position in the tail turret, I would frequently be unaware of action going on outside my field of vision. On our second mission, for example, I had not seen Lt. Cooper's plane, flying next to us off our right wing, shot down. On this fifth mission, although I had seen no enemy planes, an FW-190 had flashed across in front of our plane, shot down the B-24 directly ahead of us, and then was itself disintegrated by one of our P-47s. The tail turret was a kind of lonely place, and I occasionally turned it to the side so that I could look back to see Pete and Hank at their waist guns. It was better than the ball turret, though. Once Shorty entered it, he was suspended below the plane in a world of his own.

On February 18 our crew was called to Col. Thompson's office and presented with the Air Medals we had earned for completing five missions. I mailed mine home a few days later. All of us, I am sure, felt a certain satisfaction that Virgil was wearing tech sergeant's stripes when he appeared before our C.O., who no doubt remembered writing out the order demoting him to private.

Quite naturally, after what Thompson had done to Virgil, he was not one of Virgil's favorite people. Consequently, Virgil could hardly contain himself when he came into our hut not long after the Air Medal presentation with this tale. He had just come from the control tower, and while he was there, a P-47 had buzzed the field, a not uncommon occurrence. Col. Thompson happened to be in the tower and, using the communications system, ordered the pilot to cease. The P-47 made a sharp turn and came back low over the tower. Col. Thompson angrily grabbed the mike and said, "This is Col. Thompson. Do not buzz the field again." The P-47 made another dive at the tower, and as the plane came down the pilot's voice came over the speaker: "I'm a colonel, I'm a colonel, I'm a colonel, too." We loved it!

John Hortenstine also could testify to Thompson's being a hard-nosed individual. When he saw John with a beard not long after we arrived in England, he growled, "I want to see you in a half-hour, and I want to see you without the beard." John reported sans beard.

One day Pete, who had become a good friend of one of the cooks, who was also Mexican, entered our hut with several large sweet onions, which he shared with us. We sat on our cots and ate the onions as if they were apples. I was skeptical when he offered me one, but found it quite good. We could have mowed the Germans down just by breathing on them.

Hank Boisclair was a heavy drinker and overindulged numerous times before the rum he had picked up in Puerto Rico ran out. After he exhausted his supply of rum, we figured he would have to limit his drinking to his trips to town, where the supply was quite limited. We were surprised, though, when he came in one evening hopelessly drunk. He was almost as limber as a rubber band. We removed his shoes and practically poured him into his bed, which was the top one of a double bunk. He just as quickly kind of flowed over the other side onto the floor, a five-foot drop. We put him back in bed, and he again flowed over the other side. Had he been sober he would have injured himself. The third time we put him in he stayed put. We later learned that he had befriended one of the cooks, from whom he had acquired a bottle of vanilla extract. Though thoroughly disgusted with him, we had to laugh at how limber he was. At least he never drank the evening before we were to fly a mission.

Hank may have obtained the vanilla extract from Tom, one of the cooks. While we were at Wendover, Shorty had come across him one evening, drunk and carrying a knife and threatening to kill the head cook, whom he hated. Shorty managed to calm Tom down and thereafter seemed to feel a certain responsibility for him, in part because Tom was also a Bostonian and an Italian. I did not care for him because of his excessive drinking and also because I did not think he could be trusted. I shared my feelings with Shorty, who said, "Oh, he's o.k." For Shorty's sake I tolerated him and tried to hide my feelings, apparently successfully, for he was always quite friendly toward me. Shortly after the incident with Hank, Tom volunteered for gunnery school, was accepted and transferred, and I thought I had seen the last of him. As it later developed, I was wrong.

On February 20 Lt. Locke came to our hut to tell us that our crew had been selected to fly a PFF plane and would be transferred to the 389th Bombardment Group as soon as the officers, engineer, and radio operator had completed the necessary four weeks of training, for which they would be transferred to the 482nd B.G. Hank, Pete, Shorty, and I would remain with the 448th for those four weeks.

The selection was a compliment to our crew. As was previously explained, a PFF (short for Pathfinder Force) plane was one equipped with radar that could "see" the target through a cloud undercast. A PFF plane would lead a formation to the target and, if it was concealed by clouds, drop a flare as a signal for the other planes to release bombs; thus, the PFF crew, particularly the officers, carried a heavy load of responsibility. As pilot, Lt. Locke might have to make decisions that would affect the success of the mission. If Lt. Hortenstine failed to plot our course accurately, we would lead a whole formation astray; or if Lt. Delclisur fell down on the job, every plane's bombs would miss the target. The Germans, of course, were aware of the importance of that lead plane, so we knew that their fighter pilots were likely to give us special attention. That aspect of being a lead crew did not appeal to me, but I was pleased that the quality of our crew had been recognized.

The next day we flew our last mission prior to the four-week split-up of our crew. Virgil woke up quite ill and coughing, and an engineer from another crew replaced him for the mission. The target was the Munster, Germany, airfield, and we carried ten 500-pound general-purpose bombs. This was at the beginning of what later became known as "Big Week" because the forecast of sustained good weather encouraged making a maximum effort to destroy German aircraft factories, which were priority targets.

On the way to the target we came under heavy attack by German fighters, both ME-109s and FW-190s, and one or the other of our crew frequently used the intercom to call attention to a fighter's location. As was customary, most of the attacks came from the front, where the bombers were most vulnerable, but I saw one FW-190 come within my range as he completed a pass at a plane behind us and to my right. Quickly estimating the lead, I fired several short bursts. The nose of the 190 dropped, and the plane began a steep glide. I watched as it went down but because of our altitude, finally lost track of it. "I downed a 190," I announced on the intercom.

"Good work!" I heard from Lt. Locke. As they should have done, the other men kept silent rather than tie up the intercom.

As we approached the target, we encountered heavy flak but escaped with only one small hole in a wing tip that we found after we landed and parked. Right after we released our bombs, the 448th was attacked by Me-109s, but our plane was not singled out, and none of the Germans came close enough for me to even bother firing any "discouraging" bursts. After ten to fifteen minutes the enemy fighters disappeared, and we made the return trip without any further excitement.

As we approached Seething, I left my tail turret, as customary, and joined Pete and Hank in the waist. I was then that I learned that we had almost lost Pete. As we were on the return trip, Hank had looked around just in time to see Pete slumped over and about to fall out the waist window. Hank grabbed him, took off his oxygen mask, knocked out the accumulated ice, and turned the regulator's control valve to pure oxygen. Pete quickly revived with no ill effects and finished the mission at his waist gun position. Thereafter I was even more careful than I had previously been about checking my mask for accumulated ice.

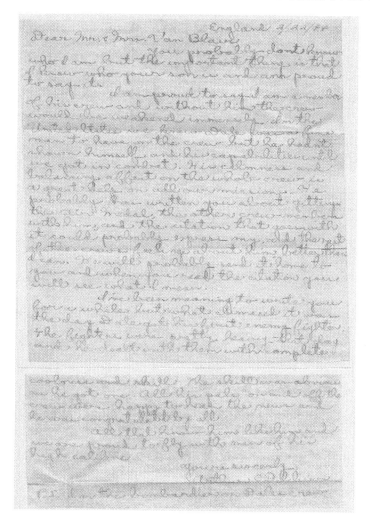

**Letter written by bombardier Arthur Declisur to the author's parents after the crew's eighth mission**

At the debriefing after the mission, a waist gunner on the crew

sitting at the table next to us overheard me as I told our debriefing officer about the plane I believed I had shot down. He immediately came to our table, said that he was on the plane next to us, and confirmed what happened. Since neither of us saw the plane crash, I received credit for a probable. As a memento, Lt. Delclisur gave me the cotter pin, together with its tag, that had been removed from one of the bombs that we dropped.

The plane flying on our right wing, piloted by Lt. Cooper, was shot down, the second time we had lost a plane flying our wing position. As was Lt. Foster's plane that was downed on our second mission, Lt. Cooper's plane was out of my field of vision. Others on our crew who saw it go down said that no chutes were seen. Because Lt. Cooper's crew was in another squadron, we did not know them.

The men of one of the crews in my hut had a harrowing story to relate when they came in. Their plane, *Bag o' Bolts*, which we had flown on an earlier mission, was hit hard by fighters over the target area, resulting in one engine on fire and another operating at only half power, electric and hydraulic systems shot out, and a fire in the waist. The pilot, Lt. Broxton, dived to ground level immediately after the bombs were released and made it back to base in spite of continued attacks by 190s. When he landed, one of the two remaining engines was burning. With no brakes, Lt. Broxton ran the plane off the runway into mud in order to stop it. The men said that their plane was riddled with bullet holes. The B-17 Flying Fortress had a reputation for getting home in spite of heavy damage, but the B-24 could take as much as the B-17. The enlisted men of this plane's crew were in my Nissen hut and were good friends. I later flew two missions with them as a replacement for their tail gunner, who was wounded on this mission.

According to the newspaper account of this mission, approximately 2000 American and British bombers carried out a day and night attack on aircraft factories, airfields and repair depots in northwest Germany. One paragraph stated, "Bombs have been hitting key targets in Germany at a rate of more than 200 tons an hour almost continuously since Saturday night. This onslaught...exceeds anything previously known in warfare...Aerial pictures...show German factories and other vital installations blown to smithereens from Rostock, on the Baltic Sea, down to Stuttgart, only about 100 miles north of the Swiss frontier." What must have been going through the minds of the Germans, both civilian and military, as they watched that stream of bombers go over?

On returning to our hut after the Munster mission, we learned that Virgil had been hospitalized with bronchitis. Shortly thereafter he was returned to the States. I very much regretted seeing him go, not only because we were close friends, but also because I had complete confidence in him as our engineer.

A few weeks after we flew this mission, Mother sent me a copy of an article that had appeared in the Quincy newspaper. The article was centered around a letter that Lt. Delclisur had written to my parents in which he told them about my downing the German fighter and what an asset I was to the crew. I was not surprised that our bombardier had written the letter, for he was that kind of a person.

# CHAPTER 9: BERLIN

When I learned that our crew would become a PFF lead crew, I was a little concerned that the four of us who were to remain with the 448<sup>th</sup> while the others were taking their month of training might be called on to fill in with other crews with wounded or sick gunners. I preferred not to have to fly with a pilot whom I did not know. However, the evening after returning from my last mission with my own crew until we were reunited at the 389<sup>th</sup> Bomb. Group, I was alerted to fly as a replacement tail gunner with Lt. Black's crew the next day, February 22. I knew nothing about Lt. Black but was, at least, acquainted with his crew's enlisted men. Our assigned target was Gotha, Germany. When take-off time came a little after nine o'clock, a low overcast necessitated an instrument take-off, a procedure that I dreaded. With the limited visibility, if a plane got a little off course, a mid-air collision could result. However, we broke through the clouds without incident and found our place at the front of the low left section. Over the continent our formation ran into rather dense clouds, and a recall was received about 1:00 P.M., together with instructions to drop our bombs on a target of opportunity. The 448th left the wing with the intention of bombing Munster, but because of a navigational error, the group dropped its bombs on Enschede, Holland, and killed many Dutch civilians. We had good fighter cover, so although we saw enemy fighters in the distance, we were not attacked. We ran into moderate to heavy flak over Germany, but lost no planes to it.

We heard that the officers of the lead plane were ordered to report to the headquarters of the 20th Combat Wing, to which the 448th was assigned, and were reprimanded. Next morning's newspaper, however, did not mention the bombing of Enschede, so the news must not have gone any further than wing headquarters. The Dutch had a government in exile that was based somewhere in England, probably London, which must have learned about the incident, but its officials probably did not want to embarrass the Allies.

According to reports, this had been one of the worst winters that England had experienced in several years. Although we had not seen much snow, it was cold and gloomy much of the time, with the kind of cloud cover that frequently caused missions to be canceled. For example, Shorty and I were alerted on three successive days, February 24-26, when the missions were scrubbed because of heavy overcast. I was glad we did not have to make the one on the 26th, for the target was Stuttgart, near the Swiss border, a long flight that gave the Germans plenty of time to put their fighters up.

On March 2 I flew my tenth mission when I filled in for the wounded tail gunner on Lt. Broxton's crew, the one which had their plane shot up on February 21 and barely made it back to base. Since the enlisted men were in my hut and I thought highly of them, I was comfortable flying with them. Our target was aircraft factories at Frankfort in central Germany. We encountered no fighter opposition on the way, but on entering the bomb run, we ran into heavy flak. Because of a rack malfunction caused by flak, the lead aircraft, which was to signal us when to drop our bombs, was unable to do so. Consequently, we flew over Frankfort without dropping any bombs. Another aircraft took the lead, and we were to bomb a target of opportunity; however, the formation was now too close to the German border to locate one. As a result, Lt. Broxton landed our plane with a full load of bombs. We found that the plane had several holes from the Frankfort flak, but no one was injured. The English newspapers reported that from 2,000 to 3,000 Liberators and Fortresses went out and met with little fighter opposition. One news article reported that it took twenty minutes for the Fortresses and Liberators to pass over their target.

A day or two later, as Shorty and I were returning to our hut after lunch, he suggested that we go into Norwich. "I'd like to buy something for Mary," he said. About two hours later we jumped off the back of the 448th truck taxi and began looking for a jewelry store. At the first one we came to, Shorty settled on a bracelet, made a down payment, and left it to be engraved, which the salesman said would take a few days. We killed the rest of the afternoon at the market and our favorite place in Norwich, the cathedral. After buying some fish and chips from a street vendor, we decided against fighting the crowd for a warm English beer and caught the truck taxi back to Seething. It was an afternoon that was destined to stick in my memory.

On March 6 I filled in as nose gunner with Lt. Sheldon's crew, a position I had not flown before. Since the nose turret was similar to the tail turret, however, I anticipated no problem. The orderly came into our hut at 3:30 A.M. to awaken us. After the usual pre-mission breakfast of fried eggs and ham, I went with Lt. Sheldon's gunners to a waiting truck that took us to the briefing room. For several days we had been expecting the first daylight mission to Berlin, and as we entered the briefing room we had the feeling that this would be it. News that a few B-17s had got to the outskirts of Berlin the previous day heightened the tension. When the briefing began and the sheet was removed from the map, there it was: a long, red ribbon stretching from Norwich to Berlin, a round trip of over 1,000 miles. The B-17s of the 1st and 3rd Divisions were to lead the way, with the 2nd Division's B-24s following, which meant we would have to be careful not to overtake the slower Fortresses. Following the briefing, we went to the equipment room to check out heated suits, flak jackets, and chest pack parachutes. Then came a trip in the back end of a truck to our plane to await take-off.

Carrying a load of incendiaries, we took off about 8:30 A.M., and because of an overcast, Lt. Sheldon had to use instrument procedure. Not having flown with him before, I was a little on edge until we broke through the clouds. After we had found our place at the front of the low left section, I prepared to enter the nose turret.

Getting into that turret required the help of either the bombardier or the navigator. To prevent a slipstream from blowing through the bombardier's and navigator's areas in the nose section, a pair of doors separated the nose turret from the plane's interior, and those doors had to be opened and then closed from inside the plane to give the gunner access to the turret. Also, the turret's own sliding doors had to be closed, which left me a little cramped for space. In the tail turret, I did not have to close the turret doors and had no second set of doors behind me; thus, if the plane were to be hit badly enough to require bailing out, I could be out of the turret in a matter of seconds, snap on the chest chute, and be ready to jump. At least I did not have the blast of cold air coming through the waist windows that I had to endure in the tail turret.

We entered Germany at 21,000 feet and a temperature of -28 degrees, a little warmer than usual. On the way to Berlin we encountered some light and inaccurate flak. We frequently sighted enemy fighters; but because of our escort of P-47s and P-51s, no attacks were directed at us or nearby Libs.

As we approached Berlin and then began the bomb run, the flak became extremely heavy and accurate, the "kind you could walk on." I would have much preferred at this point to be in the tail turret for two reasons. First, the flak bursts I saw from the tail turret were behind me and posed no threat, whereas in the nose turret I could see the heavy flak ahead and had to anticipate flying through the barrage. Second, as noted above, I could not get out of the turret without help from inside. Although I knew the enlisted men of Sheldon's crew, I did not know either the navigator or the bombardier, one of whom would have to open the doors behind me; therefore, I was a little concerned that, if we had to jump, they might not take the time to let someone they did not know out of the turret, especially if their lives depended on their getting out of the plane in a matter of seconds.

That concern became very real when I saw a group of four flak bursts right at our level and then another one a little closer. The third one was close enough that I could see the angry red flash that preceded the puff of black smoke, followed by another group of four.

Each new burst came closer and closer until I was certain that the next one would get us. We continued on the bomb run, however, with nothing more than the continuous sound of the shock waves from the flak explosions on the plane's aluminum fuselage, something like a hard wind-blown rain on a metal roof. At no time during the bomb run was there a slackening in the flak. How I welcomed the sound of the bombardier's "Bombs away!" and the turn of the formation to begin the trip home. I had been through some heavy flak on previous missions, but I had never had a feeling that I thought could be labeled fear, primarily because the flak bursts I saw behind the plane posed no threat. During that bomb run, however, I learned what fear felt like. I was ready to return to the tail turret where I did not worry about what I did not see. Because the 20th Combat Wing, with which we were flying, was the last to bomb Berlin, we received special attention from the flak batteries, which followed us with their salvoes because there were no planes behind us to demand attention. Finally we drew out of range, and the sky ahead cleared of the black puffs of smoke.

After leaving Berlin we let down to 14,000 feet and made the return trip without incident other than flying through an occasional moderate flak barrage. On examining the plane after landing at Seething about 4:15, we found numerous flak holes in the fuselage and were extremely fortunate to escape with no casualties. According to the mission report, one 448th plane was hit by flak over Berlin and was seen to head in the direction of Sweden. We learned later that the B-17 formations ahead of us encountered heavy fighter attacks. The 8th Air Force sustained a record loss of 69 planes (ten percent of the 700 B-24s and B-17s that were sent out), with over 100 others heavily damaged. The B-24H that we flew overseas cost a little over $300,000. Assuming that a B-17 cost about the same, those 69 planes cost approximately $20,700,000. Also, 690 men went down with the planes, a small percentage of whom would have survived by parachuting.

The evening of March 7, Shorty was alerted to fill in the next day on Lt. Binks's crew, whose gunners were in our hut and whom we knew quite well. As we were getting ready for bed, Shorty handed me the claim card for Mary's bracelet. "If anything happens, will you see that Mary gets the bracelet?"

"Of course," I responded. "But nothing's going to happen, and I'll be waiting for you at Binks's hardstand to return the card."

When it came close to the time for the planes to return late that afternoon, I went to the hardstand assigned to Binks's plane and waited to greet Shorty, as I had done the first time he had filled in on another crew. He had also met me when I substituted. I saw the 448th formation approach and circle the field and then watched as one plane after another landed and parked, but none pulled into Binks's hardstand. I waited for an hour in hopes that the plane would show up, then began the walk back to our hut. I was very worried but maintained hope that the plane, for some reason, had parked at another hardstand or perhaps had made an emergency landing at another base, as sometimes happened.

When I returned to the hut, no news was available. The word came a little later: Shorty's plane had ditched in the North Sea and only two of the crew had been picked up by the Air-Sea Rescue. Shorty was not one of them. I was shocked. Not wanting to cry in front of the other men, even though I knew they would understand, I rushed outside, where it was now dark, went for a walk, and let the tears come. The darkness was a perfect match for the way I felt. How could I return to the hut and his empty cot beside mine? It had to be faced, however, so after about an hour of walking the empty streets, I returned. As I walked past his cot to mine, I glanced at the shelf above his cot. There sat the photo of Mary, his fiancée. The tears came again. Several of the men came and sat around me, not saying much, but letting me know that they sympathized. I didn't sleep much that night. As many others can testify, the bonds forged in service could be strong. While there were no blood ties, Shorty had nevertheless become my brother. Even after all these years, the recollection of that day brings sadness and a sense of loss.

The two men who were picked up, Sgt. Jim Hood and Sgt. Jim Nugent came by our hut after being released from the hospital on March 14 and told me what had happened. With fuel tanks punctured by flak, they had insufficient gas to make England. As Lt. Binks attempted to ditch, a wave caught the nose of the plane, which broke in half at the bomb bays. The back half, where Shorty was, sank immediately, trapping all who were in it, and the front half went down very quickly. The top turret broke loose and trapped Nugent, the radio operator, who was several feet below the surface before he managed to free himself and go through the escape hatch in the top of the radio compartment. When he surfaced, he saw his pilot, whose Mae West had not inflated. Jim tried to swim to him, but he went down before Jim could reach him. Hood, the engineer, was standing between the pilot and co-pilot and was thrown through the windshield, but sustained only minor injuries. Hood and Nugent saw their co-pilot trying to inflate his Mae West, then he, too, went under. The British Air-Sea Rescue service picked up the two men. Neither flew again, and they were returned to the U.S.

The next morning, March 9, I was again called on to fill in as a tail gunner, this time with Lt. McCune's crew, whose gunners were in my hut and had requested me as a replacement for their wounded tail gunner. I appreciated their confidence in me but would have much preferred not to have been flying that day, partly because the target was again Berlin, but also because of being depressed. Throughout the lengthy mission, Shorty was on my mind, and I dreaded returning to his empty bed beside mine. Also, I no longer felt all that optimistic about completing the remaining missions of my tour of combat.

Based on what I now knew about the chances of a crew's successfully completing thirty missions, the odds were stacked against me. Our assigned position at the lower left corner of the formation did nothing to encourage me, either, for it was a position frequently subjected to fighter attacks. For the first time, I left without feeling that I was certain to return.

After taking off about 9:00 A.M., Lt. McCune had to follow the instrument procedure to climb through an overcast until we broke through it at about 8000 feet, at which time I entered the tail turret. After the formation had assembled and begun its trip to Berlin, I got a glimpse of the coast of England through a break in the clouds and wondered if I would see it again.

On the way to Berlin we ran into considerable flak at one point, which surprised me, for our course was usually plotted to avoid heavy concentrations of flak along the way. I found out later that our lead plane, for some reason, did not follow the prescribed course and took us over Hanover and its anti-aircraft batteries.

As before, the Berlin flak was intense and put numerous holes in the plane but did no serious damage and wounded no one. We ran into a 10/10 cloud cover over the target area; and because of equipment failure on our PFF lead plane, we were ordered to jettison our bombs, which we did in the vicinity of Nienburg. Throughout the mission, our own fighters were everywhere, and the Germans stayed on the ground, possibly because they had suffered heavy losses to our escort on March 6 and 8. On approaching Seething, we found a 10/10 undercast, which necessitated an instrument letdown. It seemed I was taking off and landing in cloud cover more often than not, and I didn't like it. Once again, though, we made it down with no problem.

According to the news reports, the 8th Air Force lost only seven bombers, all to flak. The Germans, who usually grossly exaggerated our losses, claimed only nine. The 448th lost one of the seven. It was last seen with a feathered prop just before leaving the coast of France and never showed up.

On returning to my Nissen hut, I found that Supply had already been there to pick up Shorty's things. I was upset because I had planned to gather his personal effects to return to his family, as we had promised each other to do, but at the same time I was relieved that I did not have to look at Mary's photo again.

178

The next afternoon I sadly went to Norwich to pick up the bracelet that Shorty had bought for Mary. I had to wipe away a few tears as I told the clerk what had happened. I paid him the balance due of seventeen shillings and then asked if he would mind getting the bracelet ready to mail, which he readily agreed to do. After returning to the 448<sup>th</sup> base, I addressed the package and took it to the base post office. I retained the receipt, which is now in my WW II scrapbook.

Shorty and I had promised each other that if anything happened to the other person, the survivor would write the family. We had frequently shared our letters from home, and several weeks previously, at Shorty's insistence, I had begun enclosing a note occasionally in his letters to Mary. She, in turn, frequently included something to me in her letters to Shorty; thus, I had come to the point of feeling as if I knew her. Writing her now was going to be one of the most difficult things I had ever done, but I wrote as much as I thought censorship would allow about what had happened.

On March 16 I flew my thirteenth mission with Lt. Broxton, again at the crew's request. I had recovered some of my previous optimism and was ready to get another of the required thirty behind me. Our position in the formation put one plane in front of us, one on our left wing, and several behind us. Although we did not have anyone flying off our right wing, our position was such that we weren't too likely to be singled out by fighters, which was encouraging. The target was Friedrichshafen, just across Lake Constance from Switzerland; in fact, we flew over a bit of Swiss area in making our approach to the target. We took off about 7:30 A.M. and landed about 5:45 P.M., the longest mission the 448th had made thus far. Heavy flak holed the cockpit and upper turret but hit no one. Fighter support was excellent, and we encountered no fighter opposition; in fact, I saw not a single German plane. Considering the number of missions which I had made, most of which had been well inside Germany, I had been fortunate in encountering relatively few fighter attacks.

That was the last mission I made with the 448th, for on the morning of March 22 Lt. Self came with a truck and driver to pick up Pete, Hank and me for our transfer to the 389th. He had our orders with him and had already cleared with 448th headquarters, so it was just a matter of our quickly packing our belongings. How I wished that Shorty were still there to be going with us. When I told Lt. Self about Shorty, he exclaimed, "But you were not supposed to have to fly with other crews!" If only that promise to Lt. Locke had been kept! Because a radar dome replaced the ball turret on PFF planes, Shorty was never replaced on our crew, nor was he replaced in my heart.

# CHAPTER 10: FOUR APRIL MISSIONS

Since the trip from Seething to Hethel, the 389th base, was a short one, we were dropped off in front of our quarters in the 564th Squadron area before noon. When we walked into our hut, Cappy was there to greet us. There were no single cots, only metal double bunks, and I chose an upper, for I figured that would be better than being awakened by someone shaking the double bunks when he turned over. It also had the advantage of having a shelf for such things as shaving kit and pictures right by my head. Once again I enjoyed being the center of attention when I brought out my sheets to make my bed. As soon as Hank, Pete and I had made our beds and stored our things, Cappy took us to the mess hall for lunch. It was good to be reunited with him, and I looked forward to seeing my pilot, co-pilot, bombardier and navigator again.

Hanging on an interior wall of one of the 389th buildings—it may have been the mess hall, but I am not sure—was a cornstalk. On inquiring about its significance, I learned that it had caught on the underside of one of the 389th planes which went on the low-level mission to Ploesti on August 1, 1942. The five B-24 groups participating in this attempt to knock out the oil refineries at Ploesti took off from North Africa and flew at a very low level in the hope of avoiding detection by the German air defenses. Of the 164 planes that reached Ploesti, seventy-three were lost.

Since another engineer had not been assigned to replace Virgil, we would have to fly with a temporary replacement each mission. We were not too happy about that, for we would have much preferred to have a permanent replacement who could get familiar with our routine and way of doing things.

The 564th was made up entirely of PFF crews. When a PFF crew was to lead a mission, the procedure when we began was for it to fly to the base of the group it was to lead the following day, spend the night there, and then take off with them the next morning. The C.O. of the group or another officer he designated went with the PFF plane as Command Pilot, meaning that he was in command of the formation.

The evening of the day we transferred to the 389th we flew to the base of the 453$^{rd}$ B.G., which we were to lead on a mission the next day. By the time we arrived over the base, it was dark. A few seconds after we touched down, the plane suddenly began to shake, and the right side dropped. The plane skidded to a quick halt, and a strong odor of gasoline permeated the waist, where I was sitting on the floor. The abrupt stop threw me against the fuselage, but I was uninjured. I jumped to my feet and exited through the waist window, which was now only about four or five feet from the ground. Fearing the plane would catch fire, I ran what I thought was a safe distance from the plane and was quickly joined by Pete and Hank, who had been with me in the waist. A few minutes later the rest of the crew came from the other side of the plane.

Lt. Locke explained what had happened. The moment we touched down, the runway lights had been turned off, and before his eyes could adjust to the darkness so that he could see the runway, he let the plane drift to the right. The right landing gear ran off the runway into deep mud and was sheared off. When the right side dropped, the tank in that wing was ruptured, letting gasoline run out. Fortunately, no fire occurred because Lt. Locke had immediately turned off the switches. Although there might be some bruises showing the next day, no one was injured. The plane, however, was so badly damaged that it had to be scrapped; thus, a new plane never made a mission because of someone's carelessness in turning off the runway lights too quickly.

As dark as it was, I do not know how anyone could have seen us run off the runway, but an ambulance and a truck quickly showed up. Since no one was injured, the ambulance left, and the truck driver transported us to a room with tables, then took Lt. Locke to the 453rd headquarters, where he called the 389th to report what had happened. No one offered to find us sleeping accommodations for the night; instead, we lay on tables or sat in folding chairs until the next morning, when a truck arrived from the 389th to pick us up. It was a long, long, sleepless night. Thereafter, no PFF crews went out the evening before a mission; instead, we rendezvoused in the air with the group we were to lead. We assumed the change was made because of what happened to us.

On April 1 we flew deputy lead[6] with the 2nd Combat wing for a mission to Ludwigshafen, Germany. We ran into very heavy flak

---

[6] The deputy (assistant) lead plane flew next to the lead plane, ready to take over if

over the target. Our #4 engine was hit and had to be turned off and

feathered[7], but our new Liberator, *Utterly Devasting,* brought us back

on three engines with no problem. Our plane's name, by the way,

came from one of John Hortenstine's favorite expressions. Because

we could not be sure of flying the same plane each mission, we did

not bother to have the name painted on the fuselage, although it

turned out that we flew this plane on all but our last mission.

Not long after we dropped our bombs and started the return trip,

Lt. Locke called the crew on the intercom. "Enemy fighters are

attacking a formation at one o'clock high. Gunners, keep alert."

Since the action was taking place ahead of our plane, I couldn't

see what was going on but kept scanning the sky behind our

Liberator. No Germans appeared, and we made the flight back to

England without any action. Those of our crew who could see the

formation under attack said that there must have been two hundred

enemy fighters that were engaged by the bombers' escort of P-47s and

---

something happened to the lead plane.

[7] In feathering a propeller, the pilot turned on an electric switch which activated a motor that turned the prop blades so that they were perpendicular to the air flow, thus eliminating most of the air resistance.

that quite a battle took place. They saw planes go down, but the action took place too far away to identify what kind they were.

This April Fools Day sortie resulted in some bad publicity for the 8th Air Force. We were following the 20th Combat Wing, for which the 448th was serving as the lead group, with Col. Thompson flying as Command Pilot on the 389th PFF plane that was leading that wing. When our navigator, John Hortenstine, and the one on the plane for which we were flying deputy lead realized that the 20th C.W. was following an incorrect heading, they advised Col. Thompson that he was off course and that we were correcting the heading for the 2nd C.W. Col. Thompson was invited to follow us but did not do so (typical of the colonel). As a result, some planes from the 44th and the 392nd Bomb Groups, which with the 448th comprised the 20th C.W. formation, flew over a section of Switzerland and dropped bombs on the Swiss town of Schaffhausen. Nazi propaganda gave full attention to the incident. An investigation was conducted the next day, and our officers were summoned to a meeting at the 2nd Air Division headquarters that included all the top brass. They gave their testimony and heard nothing further. We never learned what came out of the investigation. We thought it ironic that the incident should happen on April Fools Day; however, the Swiss did not think it funny. The U.S. issued an apology and paid several million in reparations.

This mission also resulted in a new commander for the 448th. According to James Hoseason's account,[8] Col. Thompson's plane ran low on gas because of severe head winds. The radar navigator and Thompson parachuted, but as the next crew member left the plane, it went into a spiral dive that trapped the rest of the crew. The navigator made it down safely, but Thompson was killed by German machine gun fire as he neared the ground. Charles C. McBride, a 448th bombardier, gives a somewhat different version.[9] He writes that the pilot, Lt. Teague, advised all crew members to bail out and then rang the alarm bell, but Teague then decided to crash land and began descending. Thompson went to the open bomb bay to jump, then returned to the flight deck. Teague advised Thompson that he had better jump, which he did. His chute only partially opened, and Thompson died on hitting the ground. According to McBride, Teague

---

[8] James Hoseason, p. 103.
[9] Charles C. McBride, *Mission Failure and Survival* (1989, Sunflower University Press), pp. 84-86

successfully crash landed and was captured, together with "several of his crew members."

When John Hortenstine and I got together at a 448th reunion in 1992, he told me that it was widely believed that Thompson was afraid to jump, hence delayed too long. At any rate, ignoring the advice from John and the other lead navigator cost him his life.

On April 8 we led the 458th at the head of the 96th Combat Wing to Brunswick, Germany, the prime target being an aircraft factory. Brunswick was an area where enemy fighters were usually encountered *en masse,* thus not on our list of preferred targets. Lt. Ken Reed joined our crew for this and subsequent missions as a second navigator. Because of the heavy responsibility placed on the navigator of a lead crew, another one would help assure that the lead crew would not lead a formation astray. This was my fifteenth mission; with its successful completion I would have half of the required thirty behind me. Except for Lt. Reed, the other crew members had five fewer than I, for neither Hank nor Pete had filled in with another crew during the time that our crew was separated for the

PFF training. I do not know how many missions Lt. Reed had made. Cappy was sick and was replaced by Dick Wallace as radio operator.

Before we took off, the Command Pilot, a colonel, handed me a pair of binoculars and said that he wanted me to keep track of the formation, the only time that I was ever asked to do so. After the formation was assembled and we were headed toward the continent, he continued calling me on the intercom to ask questions about the formation. His frequent questions were no problem until we got over the continent, when my primary concern was watching for enemy fighters, which was complicated by its being one of those days when our bombers were leaving heavy vapor trails. Enemy planes would sometimes try to sneak up on a formation by hiding in the trails. His frequent questions were a distraction, and I began to get frustrated, and the more frustrated I got, the less in awe was I of the rank of colonel. Finally, after another call for a time-consuming count of the Libs within my view, I said as respectfully as possible, "Sir, I cannot keep track of the formation and keep an effective watch for enemy fighters." He made no more calls.

As we approached Germany, enemy fighters appeared in force and ganged up on a group off to our right. I needed to be keeping a lookout for Germans in our area, but I found it impossible to take my eyes off the besieged group for more than a few seconds at a time. Fascinated, I watched first one, then another plane go down, most of them in flames, but could not tell for sure if all were ours. Altogether, seven went down. I saw no parachutes, but the formation may have been a little too far away for me to see them. I fearfully waited for our turn to come, but for some reason we escaped, even though I saw none of our escort fighters. We did not escape the flak, however. As we began the bomb run, the flak began coming up. As I reached back to pick up my flak helmet from behind the turret, I heard a tinkle of plexiglass. I looked up and saw a half-inch hole in the plexiglass top of my turret. One piece of flak had come through my turret directly above where my head normally was, but because I was leaning back at the time to pick up my flak helmet, I escaped what could have been a fatal wound. Because the flak helmet was heavy and uncomfortable, I wore it only when we ran into antiaircraft fire. That time I waited almost too long to put it on.

As we continued on the bomb run, we ran into very heavy flak. I was glad to be in the tail turret, where I didn't have to look at what was ahead of us. At any moment I expected to hear an announcement on the intercom that someone had been wounded or that we had sustained major damage, but it remained silent until I heard Lt. Delclisur announce, "Bombs away!" We led the formation in a wide turn away from Brunswick, and I thankfully watched the little, black clouds of smoke that marked the bursts of flak recede in the distance. The flight back to Hethel was uneventful.

When we returned from the mission, I was apprehensive that the Command Pilot might be irked at what he might perceive as an impertinent comment to him over the intercom about watching the formation. I expressed my concern to Lt. Locke and asked him to return the binoculars to the colonel. "Don't worry," he said; "he won't say anything." He did not.

Although our formation was not attacked by enemy fighters over Brunswick, others were, according to next morning's newspaper. One paragraph from the newspaper which I bought and saved read: "In the Saturday raids, the bomber force which hit Brunswick's airplane factories bore the brunt of the Luftwaft's defenses and suffered the heaviest losses—30 bombers. In the furious air battles that raged above the city, U.S. fighters—P-38s, P47s and P-51s—shot down 83 aircraft. One fighter pilot said he had never seen the enemy attack with such numbers and such determination." We were very fortunate not to have been involved in the air battle.

The following weekend our crew received weekend passes, and Pete and I took the train to London on Friday. This time we were able to rent a room at the Regent Palace Hotel by Piccadilly Circus for Friday and Saturday. As we wandered around looking for a good restaurant in which to eat dinner, we came to one that looked like a good possibility. On entering, we realized that we were in a rather ritzy restaurant, but we both had enough money that we decided to give it a try. On looking at the menu, we found that the prices were a little high but well within our means. The restaurant featured Continental dishes. I no longer remember specifically what I ordered, but it was a French dish that was the best meal I had during my stay in England. As I expected, Pete ordered something Spanish, which he said was also very good. That evening we went to see "Life on the

Mississippi," with Frederic March, a film based on the Mark Twain book with the same title. The film had lots of Twain humor in it, and Pete and I frequently found ourselves laughing a second or so before the English. They seemed to be just a little slow to react to his type of humor.

We had been back in our room only a short time when we saw the beam of a flashlight shining on the outside of the one window in our room. A bobbie or an air raid warden on the street below was calling our attention to our failure to pull the black-out shade. London was frequently being hit by buzz bombs at this time. A buzz bomb was basically a small, unmanned bomb with wings and an engine, aimed and launched by the Germans from the Pas de Calais area on the French coast. The engine was set to turn off at a given time, which would let the bomb descend and explode. They could not be successfully aimed at a small target such as a factory or airport, but they could be aimed at cities. We had no more than gone to bed about eleven o'clock after pulling the shade than the air raid siren began sounding. We dressed and went down to the ground level, where we waited for about three hours before the all clear sounded about 2:00

A.M. Fortunately we had the luxury of sleeping late Saturday morning.

After eating lunch at Rainbow Corner (the Red Cross Center) on Saturday, Pete and I decided we would take the afternoon to visit Westminster Abbey, St. Paul's Cathedral and the Tower of London. The taxi tour we had taken on our first trip to London had only allowed us about fifteen minutes each in Westminster and St Paul's and had stopped in front of the Tower of London for just about five minutes while the driver told us a little about its history. With the entire afternoon before us, we would be able to take a more leisurely tour of these three places. At Westminster, the first place I headed for was Poet's Corner, where such literary giants as Chaucer, Dryden, Tennyson, Dickens and Kipling are buried. We were disappointed in not being able to go into Henry VII Chapel and Elizabeth 1 Chapel, where other royalty in addition to those two are buried. Those areas were sandbagged to protect them from bomb damage and closed off to the public. The Coronation Chair and Stone of Scone had been removed for the same reason. At St. Paul's Cathedral we climbed the steps to the Whispering Gallery, which circles the base of the huge dome, second in size only to that of St. Peter's in Rome. Words whispered on one side of the Gallery can be heard on the opposite side, which is 112 feet away. When we arrived at the Tower of London, it was closed, but we spent time walking around it and seeing what we could from the outside.

That evening we went to the Coliseum to see the stage production of "Something for the Boys," with music by Cole Porter. As with "Something in the Air," which we had seen on our first trip to London, both the stars, Evelyn Dall and Leigh Stafford, were English and unfamiliar to us. Both had excellent voices. Only two of the songs had achieved any degree of popularity, the title song and "Hey, Good Lookin'," the latter of which had become rather popular before we left the States.

After we were back in our hotel room and had just lain down, the air raid siren once again sounded. This time we decided to take our chances and remained in bed. Even though we heard one hit a few blocks away, we chose our beds over the lobby of the hotel. We figured the odds were at least a thousand to one against one hitting the hotel. Besides, we thought we were far enough from the top floor that if one should hit, we probably would be safe. What it boiled down to was that we were rationalizing our way out of spending another three hours in the lobby. Many years later when my wife and I were in London, an English lady who was a baby during the war told us, "Mum took me to the public air raid shelter one time. I cried all night and she said that was it. We'll stay at home and take our chances of dying in bed." I guess her mother's thinking was somewhat like ours: faced with an unpleasant alternative, we'll take our chances.

Thousands of Londoners spent their nights in the "tube" or "underground," as they referred to their subway system. They brought blankets and slept on either cots with wire springs or the walkways. When Pete and I took the tube back to the hotel late each evening, we found hundreds of people sleeping there. I developed a great deal of admiration for these people who could spend their nights under such conditions and then put in a full day's work. Although the blitz was long since over, now Londoners were contending with the buzz bombs. When I saw the evidence of the damage done during the German aerial blitz of 1940, I marveled that the Londoners' morale did not break. The whole area around St. Paul's Cathedral, for example, was practically leveled, as were many other areas. In spite of all the bombs that were dropped around St. Paul's, the cathedral was struck by only one bomb. That one went through the dome but failed to explode, and the relatively minor damage was quickly repaired.

When Pete and I returned to Hethel Sunday afternoon, we learned that we had missed some excitement. A few German fighters had managed to sneak in as some of our planes were landing following a mission, shot up two or three and strafed the field. What an opportune time to be on leave!

When Pete received a box from his wife or parents, without fail peppers of some kind were included. Mexicans, of course, are noted for their love of hot stuff, and Pete was all Mexican. Those peppers were like candy to him. He always tried to persuade me to try one when he received a box, but I steadfastly refused. Finally, he began to wear me down. He opened a container of peppers from a box he had just received, tasted one, then said to me, "These are really mild. Come on, try one. You'll like it." He held a small pepper out toward me, and against my better judgment, I took it.

"Just chew it up and swallow it," he advised me.

I knew better than to do that. I took one bite, and that was enough. "Pete, if that is a mild one, I'd hate to taste a hot one." Pete smiled and happily ate another one. How he could eat those things without so much as blinking his eyes was beyond me.

One Friday when Pete, Cappy, Hank and I went to the mess hall for the evening meal, the Catholic chaplain, Father Beck, was standing at the entrance and reminding all the Catholic men that they were not to eat meat. I do not remember what meat was served, but it was better than usual. Pete obediently abstained, while we other three rather obviously enjoyed it. We finished our meal, and when we left the mess hall, Father Beck was gone. We were perhaps half way back to our hut when Pete suddenly exclaimed, "I'm going back and have some meat!" He made an about face and returned to the mess hall, while Cappy, Hank and I continued back to our quarters. During the remainder of our time together, we took delight in occasionally teasing Pete about his lapse and threatened to tell Father Beck, who was well-liked by Protestants as well as Catholics. He frequently came to our hut to chat. He once brought boxing gloves with him and sparred with one of the Catholics in our hut. He held his own quite well. Although he never played poker with us, we heard that he enjoyed winning money from the officers and losing it to the enlisted men.

The *Stars and Stripes* was a newspaper published by servicemen for distribution to servicemen, with each theater of operations having its own edition. In an early April issue published in England, an article with the headline "8 Fliers Adrift For Two Days In the Channel" caught my eye. I was surprised to discover that the article was about the 448th crew with whom I made my ninth mission on February 22. On April 1 they were forced to ditch shortly after crossing the French coast on the return trip. The co-pilot was lost, but the other nine of the crew survived the ditching and got into two life rafts that the radio operator, Eugene Dworaczyk, went back into the plane to release. The article reported that the crew spent "forty-two hours adrift in the English Channel…, burying their dead with improvised religious services, rowing hour after hour soaked to the skin, with only their parachutes to protect them from the biting winds and with only a little candy for food."[10]  The engineer died and was buried at sea after one of the gunners read a mass from his Catholic prayer book.  After the crew had paddled from near Dunkirk, on the French coast, almost to the English coast, they were finally spotted by the crew of an English fishing boat and picked up.  Only one who has experienced the cold of that water, as I subsequently did, can begin to realize how miserable those men were during their two days in the life rafts.

On April 12 we had to abort because of mechanical problems, but the next day we flew deputy lead for a mission to Oberphaffenhofen in Germany. J. M.  Byrd filled in as our engineer.  Our flight pattern took us near Lake Constance on the Swiss border and over beautiful snow-covered mountains.  With no cloud undercast, I watched the bombs hit the target and explode in a good pattern among hangers and a repair depot for DO-291s.  Although the flak was heavy and accurate, our plane escaped damage.  I saw only one enemy fighter, an ME-109.

---

[10] I saved the article, which is in my scrapbook.  The date of 4/10 is penciled at the top, which is probably the date of the issue in which the article appeared.

The headline in the newspaper that I bought the next morning (a newsboy came around selling papers each morning) read, "4,000 Planes Batter Nazis in 9 Countries." The 4,000 included American and British bombers based in England, American bombers based in Italy, and Russian bombers. The destruction inflicted on England during the Battle of Britain, when Germany tried to bomb England into submission or at least soften it up for invasion, was minor compared to what Germany was now receiving. The paper also reported that between 500 and 750 8th Air Force bombers were escorted by over 1000 fighters. No wonder the German pilots left us alone. This fighter cover was a marked contrast to that of the early missions we had flown, when it was frequently somewhat thin.

About the middle of the month I received a letter from Mary telling me that Tom, the cook whom Shorty had befriended and who had been transferred from the 448th to train as a gunner, had written her that he had learned for sure that Shorty had been picked up by the Germans and was alive and well as a prisoner of war. I assumed that Tom had learned of Shorty's death through corresponding with a 448th friend. His letter to Mary, of course, was a lie. I had never been as angry with anyone as I was with him. Mary was ecstatic, and I felt sick when I thought of how she and Shorty's family would feel at having their renewed hopes for him suddenly dashed. Fortunately, since Mary thought I might want to write Tom, she had included his address in her letter to me. I immediately wrote him that I knew he had lied, that his lie meant that Mary and the family would ultimately have to face the fact of Shorty's death a second time, and that unless he wrote Mary the truth without delay, I would file charges against him.

Since Tom was with a bomber group in England, I heard from him in a few days. He said that his motive was to make the family feel better, admitted that it was a mistake for which he was sorry, and promised to write Mary immediately. He kept his promise, for it was not too long before I received another letter from Mary confirming receipt of Tom's confession. She was heartbroken but agreed it was best to know the truth. I always suspected that Tom's real motive, whether he recognized it or not, was centered in a need to receive attention, to feel important. I have trouble believing that he could not have realized that what he was doing was not in the family's best interest. I should have notified his C.O. of what he had done, but did not. Since all outgoing mail was censored, I thought possibly the censor might report the situation, but I heard nothing further.

My seventeenth mission came on April 18, when we led the 20th Combat Wing (93rd, 446th and 448th) to bomb the Arado Flugzeugwerke aircraft components factory at Rathenow, just 45 miles from Berlin. Our approach to the target took us over the outskirts of Big B. With no undercast again, I observed good hits on the target. Next morning's newspaper reported that 1500 to 2000 bombers and fighters went out and that some air divisions had three-hour battles with up to 200 Nazi fighters, but I saw not a single one. In addition, the flak was light, which was highly unusual in the Berlin area. Thirteen more missions like this one would be welcome but not likely. According to the book *Tales to Noses over Berlin* by Ray Bowden, 776 B-17s and B-24s went out, with 19 being lost to flak and fighters, only two of which were B-24s.[11] The northern part of Germany had evidently been hit hard yesterday, for I saw city after city still burning on our way to and from our target.

---

[11] Ray Bowden, *Tales to Noses over Berlin,* pp. 44-45.

On April 22 the Eighth flew a mission for which we were not alerted, and as it turned out, I was glad to be on the ground. Uncertain weather conditions caused a delay in dispatching the planes, enough that the return to base was not scheduled until darkness fell. Taking advantage of the lack of light, twelve to fifteen German planes followed the Liberators back to England undetected, and as many of the B-24s were entering the landing patterns, the Germans attacked. Confusion reigned among the surprised bomber crews as they saw the first planes go down burning. Norwich anti-aircraft guns mistakenly downed one Liberator. Five bases were bombed or strafed, but Hethel escaped. In addition to the one destroyed by the English, nine were shot down or destroyed in crash landings, two more were bombed and shot up, and nine more were damaged in the air. In terms of personnel, thirty-eight men were killed and twenty-three wounded.[12]

---

[12] Hoseason, pp. 108, 110

# CHAPTER 11: BACK TO BERLIN

On the morning of April 29 we were briefed for a mission to Berlin as deputy lead for the 466th Group leading the 2nd Combat Wing. Not counting the mission of April 18, when we flew over the outskirts of Berlin, it would be my third time over the heart of the city, the first for the rest of the crew. Our target was the Friedrichstrasse rail station in the middle of Berlin, the center of the main rail and underground system networks. On arriving at our plane, I was introduced to Lt. John Bloznelis, who had been added to our crew as dead reckoning navigator. Lt. Hortenstine would continue as the Mickey (radar) navigator; Lt. Reed, as instrument navigator. Because an engineer had never been assigned to our crew to replace Virgil and because Cappy had said he was sick when he was awakened, we had two substitutes: Sgt. Harold Freeman as engineer and Sgt. Richard Wallace as radio operator. Also flying with us was Capt. Ralph Bryant, operations officer for the 786th Squadron of the 466th.

This was the thirteenth mission for the other six members of our original crew; and as we stood around on the hardstand awaiting taxi time, though not superstitious, I joked with them about my having to sweat out two "unlucky thirteenth" missions: mine on March 16 and theirs. I should have known better.

The mission began ominously, for shortly after we became airborne, our plane developed generator problems. Normally we would have returned to our base; but the lead plane had run into problems. In doing research on this mission, I corresponded with the Command Pilot on the lead plane, B. E. Steadman, who I believe was C.O. of the 466th. He explained what happened. Their problems began with a fire at the radio operator's station as they were waiting for clearance to take off. After they had taken off in a replacement plane, two or three of the smoke bomb markers began smoking heavily and had to be salvoed into the North Sea. The lead crew returned to the 389th base and took off in a third PFF plane. As they were attempting to overtake our formation, two generators went out. At that point Col. Steadman radioed us that he was aborting and that we should take over the lead. Thus, even though we also had generator problems, we had no choice but to continue, with Capt. Bryant now becoming the Command Pilot.

After the 466th formed behind us, we crossed the North Sea and Holland. Shortly before we entered Germany, our formation was attacked by FW-190s that were driven off by our fighter escort after about ten minutes. About twenty minutes later we were again hit by 190s, but again our escort of P-51s discouraged them, destroying at least one that I saw go down. We had come through two fighter attacks without undergoing an attack on our plane. I hoped our luck would hold out. Those two encounters left me on edge and encouraged me to keep an especially vigilant lookout for enemy planes. I kept my eyes and head moving, up and down and from one side to the other.

As we approached Berlin, Lt. Delclisur reported that not enough power was being generated to operate the bombsight properly and that we would have to bomb by radar, even though there was not enough undercast to interfere with the more accurate visual bombing. Immediately upon entering the bomb run we ran into intense flak. One shell scored a direct hit but, fortunately, was a dud. Instead of exploding on contact, it put our #3 engine out of commission and exited through the top of the wing, leaving a gaping hole. If the shell had exploded, the wing would have buckled and our plane would have gone down. I've often wondered if some slave laborer had sabotaged that shell. In the few minutes we were over Berlin, our plane was hit several other times, but none of our crew was wounded. Luck was still with us.

Our luck ran out, however. The disabled engine was leaking gasoline, which could result in our running out before getting back to England. Then, just after Lt. Delclisur released the flare that signaled the other planes to drop their bombs, our generators went completely out, leaving us with no power for gun turrets, radio, intercom, and other electrical equipment.

Not long after turning away from the target, we were again attacked by a group of FW-190s and a few ME-109s. Since we were caught without fighter support, the Germans were free to give us their undivided attention. One flew by so close to me going from front to rear that I thought I might recognize the pilot if we ever met again. The loss of intercom and my limited view from my tail turret kept me ignorant of the engine problems and leaking gas; however, I knew we must have problems besides the loss of electrical power when I saw that we had dropped back to the rear of the formation.

The loss of power for turrets was a major concern to me. After going through the simple procedure for converting to hand cranks and foot firing pedals, I practiced maneuvering the guns and turret. As I already knew, the emergency system was a far cry from the hand control that activated the hydraulic system. Using the hand cranks, I could not turn the turret and elevate or lower the pair of fifties nearly fast enough to track any German plane that came into my view. The German that had attacked from the front and flown by so close to me had zoomed out of range long before I could do anything. Had my turret been operating normally, I'd have had a good chance of downing him. Fortunately, none of the enemy made a direct attack on our plane from the tail except for one FW-190 that started my direction but swerved when I fired. I triggered a burst occasionally, primarily in the hope that the Germans would think my turret was functioning properly and stay clear. The front and top turret gunners were also operating their turrets manually and doing their best, along with the waist gunners, to fend off the Germans, most of whom were attacking from the front.

I watched as one of our planes slowly dropped further and further behind our formation. I knew what was going to happen. If a plane that had been hit could keep up with the formation, it had a fair chance of getting back to its base because of the protection it received from the guns on nearby planes; the Germans, however, were almost certain to gang up on one that fell behind. Sure enough, as soon as the bomber was out of range of the guns of the planes at the back of the formation, three FW-190s attacked it and quickly sent it down in flames. Then another B-24 began lagging behind and met the same fate. Since they were 466th planes, there was no chance of my knowing any of the men who went down with them. I was thankful for that but still grieved for them and their families. Twice more within fifteen minutes I watched the same tragic drama played out. I saw not a single chute come out of any of the four. That's us if we cannot stay with the group, I thought, and anxiously kept an eye on the nearest Lib to see if we were dropping behind. After a few minutes, I was much relieved to note that we had maintained our position. Twenty to thirty minutes later, however, I discovered that I could see no other planes. We were no longer with the formation. I had seen no Germans for a few minutes, though, so perhaps we would make it. It wasn't to be. Because of my limited field of vision, I didn't know that two German fighters had attacked from the front and had punctured a gas tank and knocked out another engine before being driven off by three P-47s.

According to the mission analysis written on May 2, 1944, at 2nd Air Division Headquarters, a copy of which I obtained in 1989, the attack that began not long after we left Berlin lasted for as much as an hour (seemed longer to me!) and cost the Division at least thirteen bombers, plus an additional six lost either to fighters or flak. Six were lost to enemy aircraft on the way in to the target, for a total of twenty-five B-24s.

When I at last saw the North Sea below us, I began to relax, for we had never been attacked after leaving the continent behind us. We had it made now. In forty-five minutes to an hour, we should be landing. I sat in my turret and watched enemy territory drop away. Then I felt a tap on my back. It was Hank. "We're going to ditch," he shouted above the noise of the wind and the engines. "We don't have enough gas to get back." After a brief moment of disbelief, I thought of Shorty and hoped I would fare better. I saw a bit of irony in the fact that the receipt for Mary's bracelet, which I had kept as a remembrance, was still in my billfold. Then I thought of my parents and was glad that they couldn't know what was going on.

I learned later from Lt. Locke that had it not been for Capt. Bryant we might have made it back to Hethel. After we lost Virgil, our engineer, from our crew, Cappy had been assigned the responsibility of seeing that we used up the gas in the wing-tip tanks first when starting on a mission and then flipping the switch to the main tanks. With Cappy missing, the routine was upset, and Harold Freeman, our replacement engineer for the mission, forgot to use the auxiliary wing-tip tanks first before switching to the main tanks until we were out over the North Sea headed for the continent. At that time Harold started to get out of his top turret position to switch to those tanks, but Capt. Bryant ordered him back to the turret to watch for fighters. It would only have taken Harold a few seconds to switch to the wing-tip tanks and then, when that gas was about used up, another few seconds to switch back to the main tanks. No fighters could have sneaked up on us in that length of time; besides, the waist gunners could see almost all the sky covered by the top turret. Following the loss of our generators, no power was available to switch to the wing-tip tanks when we ran low on gas. I don't doubt that Capt. Bryant, in his own mind, felt justified in what he did, but had he not interfered, we would probably have had enough gas left in the main tanks to get us back to England, for using up the gas in the wing-tip tanks as we crossed the North Sea on the way to Berlin would have conserved gas in the main tanks. As Command Pilot, Bryant was commander of the formation, but not of our plane, which was Lt. Locke's responsibility. Bryant had no business interfering with Harold.

After Hank brought me the bad news, I went back to the waist section to help throw all removable equipment—waist guns, ammunition belts, parachute packs, etc.—out the waist windows. With no power for the radio, we could send no SOS; however, firing up flares calling for fighter support brought two P-47s to us. Using hand signals, we tried to convey that we had to ditch and that our radio was out. They signaled that they understood and flew with us until the time came to hit the water.

The waist was considered the least desirable ditching position because of the B-24's tendency to break behind the bomb bay, as happened with Shorty's plane. Because there was not enough room, however, for all of us on the command deck, the area just behind the pilot's and co-pilot's seats, four of us remained in the waist: Lt. Self, Pete, Hank and me. We stretched the ditching belt and fastened it on each side of the fuselage. We then sat facing aft with our backs against the ditching belt and our hands with fingers locked behind our heads. As we waited for Lt. Locke to set the plane down, I prayed that we might get through the ditching safely and be rescued. I knew that I had no right to expect Him to answer the prayer of a backslider like me; nevertheless, I prayed. I was aware that the Liberator was a difficult plane to ditch successfully and the rate of survival for crew members was rather low (I later learned that it ran only about one out four); however, even though I dreaded the prospect of ditching in the frigid North Sea, I believed I would survive. I was still an optimist.

When Lt. Locke dragged the tail of the plane in the water to slow it prior to setting the plane down, the escape hatch flew open and icy water sprayed us. It was unbelievably cold. Lt. Self jumped up from where we were sitting on the floor between the two waist windows (a rather foolish move, I thought) and tried unsuccessfully to slam the hatch shut with his foot, then sat down again. Seconds later when Lt. Locke attempted to set the plane down, a large wave caught the nose. It was like slamming into a concrete wall. The plane broke behind the rear bomb bay, and I found myself instantaneously submerged in the frigid water without even having time to take a deep breath.

As I fought to get back to the surface, my forehead slammed against a metal object so hard that I thought I might be seriously injured. My lungs were demanding air, and I thought, I'm going to drown—what is it going to feel like? I even remembered reading somewhere that drowning was not such an unpleasant way to die and hoped it was true. I felt that I could not hold my breath one more second, yet somehow I did. At that instant my head broke above the surface, and I gratefully gulped in air. It was almost like being brought back from the dead—seconds after I had faced an imminent death, life was handed back to me, at least for the moment. I still had a chance of surviving.

I was still inside the waist section, which had not broken completely free of the forward section. If it had, I would have gone down with it. Seeing that the right waist window was completely blocked, I turned to the other window, where Pete was struggling to get through the half of it that was not covered by wreckage. For a few seconds I tried unsuccessfully to force my way through a narrow gap in the tangle of aluminum, then dropped back into the water. I thought about pulling the compressed air cylinder cords to inflate my Mae West, but stopped on thinking that I might have to dive beneath the surface in order to get out. In retrospect, I am surprised that I could swim with all the clothes I had on, which included heavy flight boots, but I do not recall having any problem. Perhaps a flow of adrenaline was the explanation. Fearing the waist section would break loose any second and sink, I frantically looked for a way out. Spotting a small opening in the side of the fuselage at the water's surface, I paddled over to it. I thankfully discovered that the fuselage had been completely ripped away beneath the water and left me plenty of room to pull myself through.

As I was about to exit through the opening, someone screamed, "Help!" I turned around but saw no one. The last thing I wanted to do was to spend any more time inside the battered plane, but I could not leave if someone needed help. Hoping that the waist section would not break loose and that the entire plane would not suddenly go under, I swam back a few feet and scanned the water, but saw no one. Pete was gone from the window. Not hearing another call for help, I swam back to the opening and pulled myself through. Once outside, I reached down to pull the cord that would cause the compressed air cylinder on the right side to be punctured, which would inflate that side of my Mae West. As I did so, I thought, what if it doesn't work? I yanked on the cord and was relieved to see that side puff up. A pull on the other cord inflated the left side, and I began paddling away from the wreckage. I feared that if the plane sank, the suction would pull me under, but it continued to float.

Hoping that someone had released a life raft, I looked around. No raft. I thought about attempting to climb up onto the wing to pull the raft release handle but was doubtful that the plane could continue to float long enough. I spotted four men in the water, but the only one close to me was Lt. Delclisur, who had a large gash over one eye with blood streaming from it. He called, "Let's stay together." I tried to swim to him but could make no progress against the waves. My arms soon felt like lead, and I reluctantly gave up. Surprisingly, the plane was still floating, and I regretfully thought that I would have had ample time after exiting the waist section to swim to the wing, climb up on it, and release the life raft. I did not see our plane sink, so do not know how long it remained afloat.

I continued to paddle around dog fashion on top of my Mae West, finding it more and more difficult to hold my head up out of the water. I was now completely exhausted, but I feared that if I turned over onto my back, the waves would wash over my head. Finally I could hold my head up no longer, rolled over, and gratefully discovered that the Mae West held my head above the water and rode me up over each wave with no effort on my part. Someone should have told us about that during our training, I thought. Having had no experience with life preservers, I didn't know that they were designed to float a person on his back.

By now, I had lost sight of everyone. I kept watching the horizon for a rescue boat, but none appeared. Never before had I felt so completely alone. Since my watch had stopped at 3:06 when we ditched, I had no idea how long I had been in the water, but it seemed like hours. One thing I was sure of: I was very, very cold, and I knew my chances of surviving were not good. I didn't give up nor panic, but I kept thinking, I don't want to die out here where my body might not ever be found. I thought of my parents and how grieved they would be to receive a telegram notifying them of my death.

Hearing the sound of an aircraft, I looked up and saw a B-24 approaching. It flew over very low with its bomb bay doors open, and I saw a man standing on the catwalk. I thought he was going to drop a life raft; however, the plane circled twice and flew off. Why didn't they do something? I was angry.

I debated whether to take off the heavy flying boots that weighted down my feet but, since the Mae West was supporting me satisfactorily, decided against removing them. If the B-24 should return and drop a raft, the boots might help retain some warmth in my feet even though they were wet. The Mae West continued to carry me up and over one wave after the other. How long, I wondered, would this ordeal go on. I suddenly realized that I no longer felt so cold and wondered why. The reason was probably hypothermia.

Then, off in the distance, I saw the most beautiful object that I had ever laid eyes on in my 22+ years: a boat heading in my direction. I later learned that Royal Marine Launch 498 had been contacted by the P-47s and given our position. As it came closer, I waved and saw someone wave back, then watched the boat pick up two of our crew. That was the last I remembered except for having, at one point, a vague sensation of someone trying to pour a bitter liquid down my throat.

Regaining consciousness was a strange experience. I was lying in a large, black tunnel. Remembering the ditching experience, I began to wonder if I were alive or dead, for there was no recollection of having been picked up. If I am dead, I thought, I must not be in hell because I do not feel either hot or tortured, but I was afraid to open my eyes. When I finally summoned the courage to do so, I found myself lying in a bunk with Lt. Locke looking at me from the bunk above.  I was alive and I was safe!  What a flood of relief I felt.

"Am I glad to see you!" I exclaimed.

He grinned.  "How're you feeling?  I was worried about you."

"Cold, but otherwise okay, I guess.  How about you?"

**Water color by Alan Rowe of an English Air- Sea Rescue launch like the one that picked up the survivors of the ditching on April 29, 1944.  Reproduced from a copy sent to the author by Mr. Rowe.**

He told me he was all right and that we were docked at Great Yarmouth and would soon be taken to a hospital.  I had been unconscious for however long it had taken the boat to pick up our crew and then cover the thirty miles from our ditching site to Great Yarmouth. I had been in the water for about an hour and was the last one to be picked up. My memory of someone trying to pour something down my throat was the result of one of the boat's crew trying to get me to drink some scotch after I was rescued. Since I had heard that twenty to thirty minutes was about as long as a person was supposed to survive immersed in the cold water, I was fortunate to be alive.

Lt. **Kenneth Reed, killed in the ditching. He joined the crew as a second navigator after they where transferred to the 389th and began flying as a lead crew**

**Lt. Arthur Delclisur, who died on the Air-Sea Rescue launch after being picked up**

Lt. Locke filled me in on what had happened to the others as we waited to be taken to the hospital. Capt. Bryant and Lt. Delclisur died of injuries and shock after being picked up. Lt. Hortenstine saw Lt. Reed with his head hanging into the water and tried to hold onto him, but became exhausted. Kenneth slipped away from him and was

225

not seen again. Lt. Bloznelis and Sgt. Freeman were never sighted, hence probably were killed in the ditching. What made Harold Freeman's death especially tragic was that he had completed his missions and was awaiting orders to return to the States when he was assigned to fill in on our crew. He had almost certainly written his parents about completing his tour, so that the word of his death would come as an even greater shock than if they thought he was still under the required number. He should not have been forced to fly with us. A few weeks later, Mother wrote me that Harold's parents, who lived about thirty miles away in Hannibal, Missouri, had contacted her to see if she could supply information about the ditching.

Lt. Self suffered a broken back and chipped shoulder bone. He later received the Soldier's Medal for freeing Pete, who had got caught on wreckage while trying to get through the waist window. It was probably Pete whom I had heard calling for help. Lt. Self had come up outside the waist window and, in spite of his injury, immediately pulled Pete loose after the one call for help. I have never figured out, however, why I did not see them when I exited through the opening in the fuselage, which was only ten to fifteen feet behind the waist window. Perhaps I remained inside longer than I realized after hearing the call for help, thus giving them time to swim away.

The other survivors had escaped uninjured or with relatively minor injuries. Lt. Hortenstine, who had been in the compartment behind the cockpit for the ditching, had covered himself with flak jackets, which had prevented his being injured when the top turret broke loose and fell on him. He was able to push the turret off and escape through the top hatch. Hank came up outside of the waist section on the opposite side from which I escaped. He lost about a half-inch from the upper left ear lobe.

Lt. Locke was knocked out by the force of the impact. When he came to, he was under the water and still strapped to his seat. After releasing himself, he escaped through a hole in the side of the cockpit and pulled the cords to inflate his Mae West, only to find that the jacket was split and would not hold air. Fortunately, an oxygen bottle floated by, which he grabbed and held on to until being picked up.

Locke later received the Distinguished Flying Cross for keeping the plane up in the formation with one engine out and for bringing it back as far as he did with two engines out. As he later said to me,

"Even if we had got back, those two engines [meaning the good ones] would never have been used again. They'd have been burned out." The last sentence of his citation, a copy of which I have, reads, "The superior flying skill and sound judgment displayed by Lieutenant Locke reflect the highest credit upon himself and the armed forces of the United States." If ever an award was deserved, that one was.

Like Harold Freeman, Dick Wallace had also completed his missions and was awaiting return to the States when summoned to fly with us as radio operator. Dick, however, escaped with no injuries.

From the Air-Sea Rescue launch we were taken to a WREN hospital in Great Yarmouth. WRENs were British women serving in the navy. The one bright spot in the whole miserable experience was being taken care of by young, pretty nurses who gave us lots of attention. The thought occurred to me that Yarmouth might be a good place to spend a two-day pass, but I found out later, much to my disappointment, that it was off limits to American military personnel.

I have no idea what my body temperature had dropped to when I was pulled from the North Sea. Although I was not told so, I assume I was suffering from hypothermia, for I shivered and shivered and shivered. The nurses put hot water bottles around me and piled blankets on me, but I continued to shake. The nurses came in throughout the night to replace the cooled-off hot water bottles with warm ones. It was nearly dawn before I finally warmed up and went to sleep.

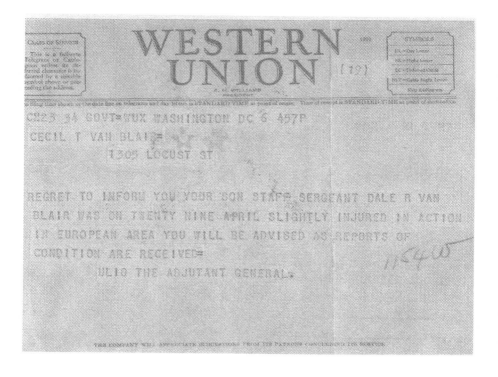

**Telegram recived by the author's parents after the ditching. Thousands of similar telegrams were sent to the families of servicemen who were wounded or killed and always began with the words "Regret to inform you..."**

About the middle of the morning a nurse came in to tell us that our transportation to the 389th base had arrived. We had to remove the pajamas that the WREN hospital had provided and wrap ourselves in blankets brought from our base for the trip back to Hethel. We were stark naked beneath our blankets. We thought the English could at least have loaned us the pajamas for the trip home with the understanding they would be returned, but apparently their regulations forbade that. Such is the nature of red tape. The clothing we were wearing when picked up should have had time to dry, but we never saw it again. Perhaps it was returned to our supply, however.

I expected to see an ambulance waiting for us outside the hospital, but instead there sat a truck, of all things. Lt. Self was the only one transported in an ambulance. That was the longest thirty-mile ride I have ever taken. I was so weak that even sitting up in that rough-riding truck was almost more than I could manage. Each time we went around a curve, I had to cling with both hands to the slatted seat to keep from falling off. I was ready to collapse by the time we arrived at Hethel.

I was put in the base hospital to recuperate, where I remained for three days. During the first day I began having a rather severe headache which aspirin did not relieve. Thinking teeth might be the problem, the flight surgeon sent me to the dentist the second day. The dentist found six cavities, which he filled, but the headache persisted. Some time during the third day I became aware of a kind of grating in the side of my head when I turned onto my left side and mentioned it to the doctor. At that point I was transported to the 231st Station Hospital on May 2, where x-rays revealed a skull fracture. The blow that I had received on the forehead had been so severe that it caused the skull to bulge enough to cause a minor fracture on the left side. In view of the sizable abrasion on my forehead, I could not understand why the doctor did not immediately suspect a skull fracture when the headache began instead of shipping me off to the dentist. The teeth needed to be filled, but that was not the most opportune time for me to have to undergo that ordeal.

Across the aisle from me in the hospital was a P-38 pilot who, when his plane had developed an engine problem on a practice flight, had bailed out and immediately pulled the rip cord instead of waiting for his body to slow down, as all flight personnel had been taught to do. The impact resulting from the chute's opening while he was traveling at such a high speed did considerable damage to the pilot, though it did not show on the outside. Immediately after I was admitted to the ward, one of the nurses dressed the abrasion on my forehead, and the pilot said in a sarcastic tone, "Is that all you're in here for?"

The nurse said to me, "Don't pay any attention to him." Of all people, he should have realized that there could be another problem that did not show. I was not aware of his background at the time or I would have replied that at least I was not in for losing my head and pulling a stupid stunt. He was the only man in the entire ward who gave the nurses any problem by demanding constant attention.

Since a truck taxi ran daily between Hethel and the hospital, less than an hour's drive, men from my hut visited me and brought my mail three or four times during my stay. After two or three days the headaches completely disappeared, and I began enjoying being a recuperating patient—no duties and nurses to give me a back rub each evening before the lights were dimmed. The day before I was released, though, I was brought back down to earth with a thud by being assigned K.P. duty in the ward's small kitchen. All it involved was running the dishes through the dishwasher, but I thought that as a staff sergeant I was forever free of that undignified labor.

On learning that Lt. Self was in the ward next to me, I went to visit him. He had two broken vertebra and was in an uncomfortable body cast, which would not be removed for about three months. He was expected to make a complete recovery.

After ten days in the division hospital, I returned to Hethel on May 11. When I entered our Nissen hut, first one man then another came bringing various items of my belongings to me, which I had rather expected to happen. When a crew was lost, the accepted practice was for other men in the hut to appropriate any items of equipment other than personal things before Supply came to take everything away. It may sound cold-blooded but really was a very practical understanding among us—we preferred for someone we knew to have an item than for it to go back to Supply. Sometimes two of us would make an agreement. For example, the man who bunked next to me, Sgt. Ziglinski, and I had an understanding that if I were lost, he got my sheets; if he were lost, I got his leather A-2 jacket. At any rate, every item that belonged to me was returned without any prompting by me. In lieu of my A-2 jacket, which had gone down with our plane, Supply issued me an English-made wool jacket that I liked very much, especially since no one else I knew had one like it. I still regretted losing my A-2, however.

The watch that I had purchased in Brazil was a casualty of the ditching. I normally wore my old watch at all times because I preferred to save the new one for post-service days, but on a whim I put on the new one the morning of the mission. By the time the personal belongings that accompanied me on the mission were returned and I was able to take the watch to a Norwich watch repair shop, the watch's works were so damaged by the salt water as to be beyond repair. It now resides in a display case of my medals and other memorabilia which my wife had made several years ago, where it provides a permanent record of the time of our ditching at 3:06 P.M.

The mission of April 29 turned out to be one of the costliest of the war: sixty-three bombers and fourteen fighters lost. Sixty-nine bombers were lost on March 6 (my first Berlin mission); sixty-four on

April 11. Thus, I had the dubious distinction of being involved in two of the three worst missions in terms of bomber losses. The total of seventy-seven matched March 6 for the number one position of total number of aircraft lost.

The chances of a combat crew member's finishing the required number of missions while I was flying were not good. According to *The 1000 Day Battle*, by James Hoseason,[13] only 27 of the original 70 crews that went overseas with the 448th completed the tour of duty. During the three months that I flew combat with the group prior to my transfer to the 389th, the group had 37 aircraft shot down, a loss rate of just over 50%. In *Deadly Sky*, John McManus observes that "by early 1944, heavy-bomber groups were incurring 88 percent casualty rates over a six-month period."[14] More men lost their lives in the Eighth Air Force than in the Marines, even though the latter had 250,000 more people. The United States Army Air Forces had the highest casualty rate of any branch of service. I wonder how many of us would have volunteered for combat crew training if we had known

---

[13] Hoseason, p. 245.
[14] John McManus, *Deadly Sky* (2000: Presidio Press, Inc.), p. 338.

this was going to be true. Given my inherent optimism and my hatred of K.P. duty, I just might have.

When one considers the many ways in which an airman could lose his life, it should be no surprise that the AAF had the highest casualty rate. He could be hit by flak or bullets from enemy aircraft. His plane could take a direct hit from flak and explode, with no one having an opportunity to bail out. Flak or fighter damage might cause a fire that sent the plane down burning, as I saw happen on numerous occasions. There was always a possibility of one's plane being taken out by a nearby plane that had been shot up and could not be controlled. A badly hit bomber frequently went into a dive or spin that trapped its crew inside. Even having time to bail out was no guarantee of survival. Parachutes could fail to open, or they may have been damaged by flak or fire. Many crew members who parachuted safely were beaten or pitchforked to death by angry civilians before the military arrived, or there was always the possibility of landing in the wrong place, such as water or isolated mountain areas. If a plane had to ditch, the chances of everyone's surviving were very slim. Accidents claimed many lives. Overloaded planes sometimes crashed on taking off; others with battle damage crashed on attempting to land. Numerous planes were lost in collisions resulting from taking off into an overcast, with the almost-certain deaths of all crew members on both planes. In view of all the ways in which an airman could become a statistic, one that finished the required missions was indeed fortunate.

# CHAPTER 12: BACK TO THE HOSPITAL

The day after my release from the hospital, I was given a choice of spending a week in the rest home or receiving a week's furlough to go anywhere I wished. It was a rather difficult decision, but I chose a week in London even though I would have to go by myself. Since our other crew members except for Cappy had left for an Eighth Air Force rest home while I was in the hospital, they were about due to return; otherwise I would have chosen the rest home so that I could be with them. Cappy was not available, either, for he was awaiting court martial. He had not gone on sick call after claiming to be sick the morning of the mission; in fact, he admitted to me that he was not actually sick but had simply decided he did not want to fly that day. He told me that he blamed himself for our ditching, for had he gone he would have taken care of switching between the wing tip and main gas tanks. His court martial resulted in his being demoted to private and sentenced to several weeks in the guard house. Cappy had previously never given any hint of being inclined to shirk duty; hence,

I felt sorry for him, though at the same time I believed it was true that we might have avoided the ditching if he had gone with us.

The seats on the train to London were all taken when I boarded it in Norwich; thus, I had to stand in the aisle. This train's cars were different from those on our first trip to London. Instead of having two-seated compartments with doors that opened directly onto the loading platform and no aisle, this one had compartments and an aisle that ran the length of one side of the car. Neither bore much resemblance to American cars with their two rows of seats and a center aisle and no compartments. The English cars were also much smaller than the American ones.

Standing next to me in the aisle was an 8th Air Force lieutenant, a pilot, with whom I struck up a conversation. I was quite surprised to hear him speak with a typical English accent. He had enlisted in the Royal Air Forces at the beginning of the war and had acquired the accent through constant exposure, according to him, but I wondered if he had worked at it. He had just recently transferred to the Eighth Air Force.

After getting off the train in London, I took a taxi to the Regent Palace hotel, only to find that no rooms were available. A pilot waiting to get his key stopped me as I turned away from the desk and said, "Would you want to share my room? I'm alone and don't mind sharing a double bed if you don't." I thankfully accepted the offer. Only a combat crew officer would have been likely to offer to share his hotel room with an enlisted man.

The lieutenant was a B-26 pilot, who referred to that twin-engine bomber as a flying coffin and related some of his bad experiences with it to me. Other than eating a meal or two together, he went his way and I, mine. He was in London for just two days, and on his departure I retained the room.

After dropping off my things in the room and talking to the lieutenant for a while, I walked the block or so over to Rainbow Corner, the Red Cross Center at Piccadilly Circus. While I was scanning through the hometown register for Illinois, a paratrooper standing beside me asked, "Are you from Illinois?" When I replied that I was from Quincy, he extended his hand and exclaimed, "Well, what do you know! I'm from Quincy, too!" Since Bob (not his real name, which time has obliterated from my memory) was in London by himself and had no plans, we agreed to see the city together during the rest of his leave.

The next morning we rode the underground to Madame Tussaud's, the world-famous waxwork exhibition founded by Madame Tussaud in 1760. Hundreds of life-like wax models of historical and contemporary celebrities are on display. After touring the exhibition, we decided to walk back to Piccadilly but were in doubt which way to go. A doorman was standing with his back to us a few feet away, so Bob stepped over to him to request information. On receiving no response, Bob tapped him on the shoulder, only to discover that he was talking to a wax dummy. Bob felt a bit like a dummy, too.

That evening, while we were eating at Rainbow Corner, one of the hostesses asked if we would care for tickets to see Bebe Daniels and her husband, Ben Lyon, in the stage production of "Panama Hattie." Both were popular Hollywood performers, and "Panama Hattie" had been a recent Hollywood movie. Miss Daniels had sent the tickets, which were for the end box that hung almost over the stage, some of the best seats in the theater. We quickly accepted the tickets and joined four other GIs, who had also received free tickets, who showed up to take the other seats in the box. During the intermission we sent a note to Miss Daniels thanking her for her thoughtfulness. At the beginning of the next act she looked up at us as she came on stage and smiled, which we assumed was her way of saying "You're welcome." She made quite an impression on six young soldiers.

Based on the training that his unit had been undergoing, Bob insisted that the invasion of Europe would take place within six weeks. On my return to the base, if I had placed some bets with others in my hut that the invasion would occur within that period, I would have cleaned up, for it came in less than a month.

After two days together, Bob's leave expired and I was left on my own. The first evening after his departure, I went to a movie and found a seat next to an attractive girl. We conversed a little in the few minutes before the movie started and then left together after it was over. I walked with her to a bus stop and debated if I should offer to accompany her home. Since she had said she lived with her parents, I didn't think she would jump to any unwarranted conclusions about my motives. However, I was fearful of running into a problem in navigating my way back via bus transportation. The alternative was a taxi, but I had no idea how far away she lived and how much a taxi might cost. Consequently, I didn't broach the subject. I waited with her until her bus came, said goodbye, and began the short walk to my hotel. Then it hit me: I hadn't even remembered to ask for her phone number. You really blew that, I thought. That was as close as I came during my time in England to establishing a relationship with a girl.

A day or two later I awoke with a headache, which I killed with aspirin. It kept recurring, and I assumed it must be the aftereffects of the skull fracture. It became more and more painful, and I returned to Hethel one day before my furlough ended. As the headache worsened, I took more aspirin and rather foolishly did not immediately go on sick call. The possibility of my having something seriously wrong just did not occur to me—my health had always been perfect. Moreover, one did not go on sick call with just a headache, I thought. Finally, on the morning of the third day after my return from London, two of my friends took me to sick call, for I could hardly manage to walk without an arm over each friend's shoulder for support.

I spent that day and night at the base hospital. Some time during the night I got up and managed to stagger to the latrine, which was just down the hall, then could not remember how to get back to my bed. The male orderly came along and saw me and led me to it. The next morning, May 20, I was returned to the hospital where I had recovered from the skull fracture. The diagnosis was spinal meningitis. I was told later that my temperature was 106°.

The next three days were bad. The high temperature, spinal taps, taking huge sulfa pills and being forced to drink glass after glass of water that I did not want but which the pills required, all accompanied by the pain that goes with spinal meningitis, made for a miserable experience. My head and my neck ached constantly, and my spine was stiff. I especially dreaded the spinal taps. I had to lie on my side, draw my knees up, and arch my back outwards. A male orderly then held me in that position so that I would not involuntarily move and cause damage when the spinal tap was taken. When the doctor inserted the needle at the base of my spine to withdraw fluid, the needle felt as if it were six inches long. There was some pain, but not a lot. It was just the feel of the needle going in that I dreaded.

Although I didn't know until a nurse told me after I was well on the way to recovery, I was also being given penicillin.

Two or three times my doctor came into my room (I was in isolation) with two other doctors and stood at the foot of the bed conversing with them in voices so low that I could not hear what they were saying. Even if they had talked normally, I probably could not have understood them because the meningitis had affected my hearing. At the time I was not too concerned about the doctors and their conference at the foot of my bed. I did not realize how critical my condition was, a case of ignorance being bliss.

As I lay there during those first days, I naturally thought about one thing after another. In my imagination, I went here and there, but most frequently I went home. The remarkable thing was how real those imaginings were. I wasn't hallucinating or dreaming, but when I thought of home, for example, it was almost as if I were there. I suppose it was an effect of my high temperature, because after it went down, my imagination returned to normal.

One of my main concerns was my lack of access to a bathroom. With all the water I was drinking, it did not take me long to fill the small urinal (we called them "ducks") that was left with me. Since there was no buzzer system for calling for help, I had to wait for an orderly or nurse to stick his/her head in the door before I could get my duck emptied so that I could begin to fill it again. On several occasions it was touch and go as to whether I would make it, but I always did.

After a few days of penicillin and sulfa, the headaches began to let up, my hearing returned to normal, and the stiffness in my spine lessened. Finally, on May 28, I was taken out of isolation and put into the ward, but was still confined to bed. One of the nurses told me that I was very fortunate to have arrived when an adequate supply of penicillin was available, for they were at times out of it. Though she did not come right out and say so, I gathered that my chances of survival would have been negligible without the penicillin, which was a relatively new "wonder drug" with limited availability. The armed forces, of course, had priority in its distribution.

The day before I left the isolation room, in talking to a nurse I mentioned that this was by far the longest I had gone without writing my parents. Since I still had not progressed to the sitting-up stage, she immediately asked, "Would you like to dictate a letter to me for them?" I gladly accepted her offer, not only because I wanted to get a letter off to my parents, but also because it gave me a few more minutes with a very nice young lady. Ever since my two stays in the hospital after the ditching, I have been ready to sing the praises of the nurses who took care of me. Not only were they capable and efficient, but also they were, without exception, cheerful and kind and frequently went beyond what they were required to do. Every once in a while, one of them would stop to ask how I felt and take time to chat for a few minutes. Then there were the nightly back rubs. How I loved those! I can't believe that the nurses always enjoyed taking the time for them, but they gave the impression that they did.

As I lay in bed the day after being put into the ward, I realized that when I turned onto my left side with my ear buried in the pillow, sounds were quite muffled. Since the illness had affected my hearing level during those first several days but then had come back, I assumed my right ear was still recovering. However, I casually mentioned my discovery to a nurse. In short order I was taken for x-rays and tests. The verdict: a dead nerve and permanent and total

248

hearing loss in the right ear. Since the left ear was still normal and I experienced no difficulty in carrying on a conversation, I was not overly concerned. I was thankful still to be alive.

I was concerned, though, when the nurse got me out of bed for the first time on May 31 and took me for a short walk. I could not walk a straight line but rather veered sharply to the left; moreover, I became dizzy and sick to my stomach. The hearing loss had upset my sense of balance. I have always had a high pain tolerance, but the dizziness and sickness I experienced on getting up was worse than pain. I dreaded it. Over my sometimes strenuous objections, the nurses, who kept telling me that this was the only way I would get over the balance problem, kept making me get out of bed and walk. As lieutenants, they outranked me, so I had no choice but to obey. As the nurses continued to get me up during the next two days, I found myself able to stay up longer and longer, until the dizziness and sickness finally disappeared. On June 3, according to a letter that I wrote to Mother and Dad, I was even able to start taking some light calisthenics. For a long time, however, I could not look up and walk a straight line.  Also, for three or four years afterward, I would occasionally get a little dizzy, but not sick.

The first news I heard on awakening on the morning of June 6 was that American and British troops had landed at Normandy.  I thought about the paratrooper I had befriended in London and hoped that he would survive.  As I listened to the Libs and Fortresses go over to bomb German positions, I regretted not being able to participate actively in this historic action.  I regretted it even more after I returned to Hethel and heard my friends tell about the hundreds of ships they saw as they flew over the Channel.

One of the men with whom I got acquainted in the hospital was an armorer on a B-24 ground crew.  One of his duties was to clean the guns after the plane to which his ground crew was assigned returned from a mission.  About a month previously he had taken the back plate off one of the machine guns in the tail turret preparatory to removing the bolt.  To remove the bolt (a block of steel about eight inches long and two inches square), the trigger mechanism had to be released.  When he did that, a fifty-caliber round that the tail gunner had failed to clear from the gun exploded and drove the bolt against the armorer's forehead. Considering the weight of the bolt and the thousands of pounds of pressure exerted against it by the explosion, he should have been instantly killed. The bone, of course, was shattered and had to be removed. By the time I met him he was up and walking around, and skin covered the injury. A plate was to be inserted in a subsequent operation.

The first Sunday after I had mastered the art of walking again, one of the nurses invited all interested men in the ward to go to church with her, and several of us accepted the invitation. It was the first time I had attended a worship service since leaving the States, and it felt good once again to attend. I now firmly believe that I survived the ditching and the spinal meningitis through the grace of God and should have changed my ways at that point, but at the time I did not bother to give Him credit. I did attend two or three worship services on the base after my release from the hospital, but otherwise showed no gratitude to Him.

By an odd coincidence, the next person placed in the isolation room where I had spent a week was a boy from Quincy who had also developed spinal meningitis (not from a ditching, however); and he, too, was a tail gunner on a Lib. I no longer remember his name, though I visited him a few times before my release.

Shortly before I left the hospital, heavyweight boxing champion Joe Louis came to visit. He did not come through our ward, but as I was outside taking a walk on a warm day, I met him and his entourage as they were going from one building to another. Must be nice, I thought, to be able to spend your time in service visiting hospitals. I was not impressed. I later saw Billy Conn, who had come very close to defeating Louis prior to entering the service, box an exhibition match at our base. That, I felt, was much more worthwhile.

One of the things that the families of servicemen most dreaded was the sight of a Western Union person approaching their home, for the War Department used Western Union telegrams to notify families that a loved one had been wounded or killed. My parents were fortunate in that they had received letters from me written after we ditched, so that when they received their "regret to inform you" (all telegrams began with those words) telegram the middle of June, they already knew that I was all right.

My goal was to be released from the hospital before my birthday on June 17. I beat that by three days. The next day, June 15, I wrote my parents about losing the hearing in my right ear but assured them that "my left ear is perfectly all right and just as good as it always was, so I can hear about as good as ever." The hearing loss, of course, meant that my flying days were behind me. As I pointed out to them, the disability might be a blessing in disguise, for before completing seven more missions, worse might have happened to me. I did, however, regret losing my flight pay.

On June 19th I was told to report immediately to my squadron C.O., Major Dale Sisson, a pilot who had completed his missions. He had been notified of my release, thus was expecting me. He looked up when I entered his office and saluted, then said, "Don't tell the flight surgeon I told you this, but he told me not to expect you back." We discussed my ditching experience for several minutes, then he told me to take it easy for a few days, after which he would have an assignment for me that would allow me to "goldbrick," i.e. get by without working too hard. I couldn't believe what I had heard my

C.O. say and concluded that the sympathy he had expressed to me about my ditching and the ensuing hospital stays was quite sincere.

A day or two later, I came close to a catastrophe. Pete and I were heading for the mess hall. As I stepped off the curb to cross a street, Pete grabbed me and pulled me back just in time to keep me from being hit by a truck. I had heard the truck and looked in the direction from which I thought it was coming, but on seeing no truck, had begun to cross the street. Because of the deaf right ear, all sound now seemed to come from the left. I was going to have to remember to use my eyes to compensate for the hearing loss.

Shortly after reporting back to the 389th, I was summoned to squadron headquarters and presented with the Purple Heart. Since I had not been hit by enemy fire, I had not given one thought to receiving the award; however, since my skull fracture and spinal meningitis were the direct result of enemy action, the powers that be said I had earned it.

# CHAPTER 13: GROUNDED

One week after my release from the hospital, Major Sisson sent for me and directed me to report to the squadron bombardier, whose office was next to Major Sisson's, for whom I would do typing and other clerical work. I had done well in my high school typing class and had continued to do enough typing after graduating to maintain a fair degree of proficiency. Though I had had no opportunity to type since entering the service, I found that my speed and accuracy had not deteriorated as much as I feared.

I enjoyed working for the squadron bombardier, whose name I no longer recall (I remember Major Sisson's name because it is on a form in my scrapbook). He was a very considerate person and easy to work for. My work was interesting, my hours were flexible, and weekend passes were easy to obtain. It wasn't exactly a "goldbrick" job but certainly was not very demanding. I was on good terms with all the officers in the headquarters building, who took me with them when they went skeet shooting. Perhaps my combat crew background and their knowledge of what I had just gone through inclined them to give me special consideration, but I doubt it. Most of them were former members of combat crews, and I always found flying officers to be considerate of enlisted men. Best of all, though, I felt secure. No more scanning the skies for ME-109s and FW-190s and no more flying through a heavy barrage of flak. No more counting missions and hoping I would make it through my tour of duty.

While I was working in the squadron bombardier's office, Col. Jimmy Stewart, now the C.O. of the 2nd Combat Wing to which our group was assigned, spent a day in our office looking over strike photos. He was a very unpretentious, likable person with an excellent sense of humor. I was so awestruck at being in his presence that I did not have the nerve to ask for his autograph. It somehow did not seem the thing to do. I have often wished that I had told him of the role that his Air Forces propaganda film had played in my volunteering for gunnery school, for I suspect he would have found it amusing. Perhaps he might even have been pleased to meet someone on whom his film had made an impact. Incidentally, I have a video of that recruiting film which my older daughter gave me for Christmas, 2001.

It's a great remembrance of a man whom I admired and who exerted a significant influence on my World War II service.

In one of her letters Mother enclosed a newspaper article about Frank Blaesing, the close friend who had shared the room with me in Rock Island. Frank, who had been intending to enlist in the Coast Guard when I left for the Air Forces, had enlisted instead in the Air Forces in January, 1943, had become a radio operator on a bomber crew, and had been killed on his first mission in Indo-China. I thought of the good times we had shared, especially the months when we roomed together in Rock Island. Now there would be no reunion after the war. Another close friend was gone.

Although flying and ground personnel were housed in separate areas, Pete and I had remained in our same Nissen hut after being grounded. Not long after I began working in the squadron bombardier's office, the first sergeant sent word for us to move in with the ground personnel. We were very upset, for we did not want to leave our friends. Moreover, we felt we had earned the right to stay with the flight crews. We packed up, however, and took a truck to the hut to which we had been assigned. Every bed seemed to be taken, and no one was in the hut to question about the bed situation. We could have gone to the first sergeant, but we were ready to rebel. "Let's go back," said Pete, to which I readily agreed.

We moved our gear back to the hut we had just left, and I went to Major Sisson with our tale of woe. "Stay where you are," he said, and we heard no more from the first sergeant. A friend told us, however, that he was rather perturbed at our going over his head. That pleased us. And I enjoyed the feeling of having a little pull in the right place, for I had never been in that position before during my service days.

After I had worked for the squadron bombardier for a few weeks, Major Sisson borrowed me to help get out some reports that were due shortly. To meet the deadline, I worked several hours of overtime, which I did not mind doing, for I liked our C.O. After the reports were finished, he summoned me to his office and said, "You've been working too hard. I'm going to make you squadron gunnery sergeant."

Naturally, I wanted to know what was involved. "What do I do?"

"Not much," he said. "Get up when we're flying a mission and go to the briefing. If a crew comes up short a gunner, go wake someone up to fill in. If you don't feel like getting up, don't worry. Someone else will take care of it."

That was my job for the duration of my time in England. Once I had gone to a mission briefing, I had no other obligations; consequently, I had more free time than I knew what to do with. To kill some of it, I began for the first time to sit in on the frequent poker games that went on in our hut. I had previously done lots of observing, hence knew more than just the basics. I did not always win, but I won often enough that I sent money home several times. I recall one evening of poker when I was having especially good luck and another player, luck that was as bad as mine was good. Finally I came up with an outstanding hand and raised the full ten-shilling ($2.00) limit we had set. The one whose luck had been running so bad raised me back, and I naturally raised him again. After two or three more raises back and forth, I finally called without raising him, partly because I felt sorry for him. The unlucky fellow laid down four kings and was about ready to commit murder when I laid down four aces. That broke up the poker game.

I also undertook to learn to play chess but never gained much skill at it. My instructor was one of the men in my hut; and while he was not a great player, I never progressed to the point of winning even one game from him.

I no longer recall exactly when Jimmy Cagney brought his U.S.O. troupe to Hethel, but I believe it was in late June. It was the best of the three or four that I saw during my eleven months in England, primarily because of Cagney himself. He sang and danced some of his numbers from "Yankee Doodle Dandy."

Lt. Locke returned to the States three weeks or so after my release from the hospital. How I envied him when he came by to bid me farewell. Lt. Self, who had been in the hospital with his broken back ever since the ditching, was finally released not long after Locke left and given his orders to return, also. Still wearing a back brace, he came by to ask Pete and me to help him pack and load his gear on the truck that was to take him to the depot, which we were glad to do. John Hortenstine dropped out of sight; and it was not until I tracked him down in the late 1980s that I learned that he had served for about three months in Intelligence, then got to thinking that, according to regulations, if he went back to flying he could collect flying pay for the previous three months. When we got together at a 448th reunion in 1992, he told me, "I got greedy and requested assignment to flying duty." He served as an instructor for crews taking PFF training and also flew eight night missions scattering propaganda leaflets behind the German lines. He remained in the Air Force reserves after the war, was recalled to duty during the Korean War and flew sixty-one missions in a B-26, and finally retired after twenty years, part of which was in the reserves, as a lieutenant colonel.

During the summer, Hank Boisclair surprised me with a visit. I had not seen him since we ditched, for by the time I was released from the hospital, he was gone and nobody had any information. I was surprised to find that he was now with the 15th Air Force in Italy and was again flying as a waist gunner on a B-24. Of our crew members who escaped without serious injury, Hank was the only one to be reassigned to combat duty. Given a furlough, he had caught a ride to England on a plane in order to visit me. Hank was missing the top part of one ear as a result of the ditching. It was to be repaired through plastic surgery at some time in the future. My ear problem at least got me grounded and out of combat. Although that was my last contact with him, I later learned that he survived his missions with the 15th Air Force. After returning to the States, I began corresponding with Mrs. Henrietta Reed, mother of Harold Reed, who was killed in our ditching, and in a letter written in May, 1945, she told me about a surprise visit by Hank, who was stationed at Atlantic City, New Jersey. He had taken the train to visit her and Mr. Reed in Ithaca, New York.

In July a letter came from Carl Eyre, my hometown friend whom I had last seen on my furlough in June 1943. He had recently arrived in England and was with a fighter squadron based about twenty miles from me, where he worked in an office. Carl suggested that we arrange to meet in Norwich some evening, which we soon did. Subsequently Pete and I frequently met Carl in Norwich, and the three of us also spent a weekend together in London. In addition, each of us got a two-day pass to visit the other at his base. It was during my visit to Carl at his base that I heard the "Warsaw Concerto" for the first time, and it immediately became one of my favorites. A Red Cross lady who worked at the enlisted men's club on his base was an accomplished pianist and played the concerto for us. One of the first records I purchased after my discharge was the "Warsaw Concerto."

During the weekend that Pete, Carl, and I spent in London, one of our trips by taxi took us by the hotel in which Pete and I had stayed in April and had decided to remain in our room when the air raid sirens sounded the second night of our stay. We had figured the chances of the hotel's being struck were too small to warrant losing part of a night's sleep. When we passed the hotel and looked up, we saw that the hotel had been hit by a buzz bomb in a subsequent air raid and that the top two or three floors had been destroyed. The three of us agreed that if the air raid sirens sounded that night, we would not let losing a few hours of sleep keep us from taking shelter.

During the summer the 389th celebrated the completion of 200 combat missions. Present were representatives from the U.S., Great Britain, Russia, Holland, Norway, Poland and Egypt. Generals Spaatz, Doolittle, and Kepner attended. The highlight of the occasion was a formation of sixty Liberators, followed by fifty Mustangs (P-51s), that flew over at 1,500 feet. There were dances and other types of entertainment and lots of food. Col. Shawki from Egypt made a hit with the enlisted men by making himself available to signing dozens of "short snorters," one of which was mine. Everyone who had crossed the equator, as I had on my way overseas, was supposed always to carry a bill with him that was signed by at least one other person—mine was an English ten-shilling note. That bill was called a "short snorter." If someone asked to see another's short snorter and he couldn't produce one, he was supposed to buy the other person a drink.

One of the big events at Hethel about the middle of August was the arrival of a soda fountain where we could buy genuine fountain Cokes. In 1943 Robert Woodruff, president of Coca Cola, had pledged that everyone in uniform would "get a bottle of Coca Cola for five cents, wherever he is and whatever it costs the Coca Cola Company." Whether our fountain cokes were part of that pledge, I do not know. What I do know is just how good those first ones tasted to us on a warm day. We had had no soft drinks since leaving the U.S.

Some time during the summer I learned that servicemen from Illinois could get an absentee ballot for the November election, applied for one and subsequently received it in late summer. I very proudly voted for the first time and marked the square in front of the name of Franklin D. Roosevelt. When I mailed it, I wondered if there was any chance of my being back in the U.S. by the time that vote was counted.

# CHAPTER 14: BACK TO THE STATES

My position as squadron gunnery sergeant could hardly have been improved on. Although it required getting up early when missions were scheduled so that I could be at the briefings in case a replacement for a crew was needed, once the briefing started I was free to leave. I didn't much like having the responsibility of selecting someone to sub, since it could mean I was sending someone to his death; therefore, I occasionally took advantage of Major Sisson's statement that if I didn't feel like getting up, someone else would take care of it. I was very fortunate, however, in never having to shoulder that responsibility during the months I served as squadron gunnery sergeant. It seemed that the men just didn't suddenly get sick during the night. The need for a replacement usually arose out of someone's being wounded on a previous mission, so that his replacement could be selected the day before a mission. For example, when I flew the five missions as a replacement while still with the 448th, I was notified no later than the evening before a mission that I would be filling in with a certain crew the next day.

267

In view of how easy I had it, I should have been content to remain in England for the duration of the war instead of seeking to be returned to the States where military service entailed petty rules and regulations, officers who too frequently felt their own importance (many of ours overseas could care less if you bothered to salute), frequent inspections (ours were a rarity), etc. Had I remained I might even have received an appointment as flight officer and become squadron gunnery officer, with more responsibilities, primarily in the area of training to hone the skills of gunners, for we heard that establishment of that position was being considered.

My one desire, however, was to get back to the U.S.; and finally, on September 9, I learned that my orders to return were being sent through. Now it was a matter of waiting for them to clear all the red tape and hoping that nothing untoward happened along the way. Sixteen days later, on September 25, the orders were placed in my hands. I was elated. Pete also received his that same day.

On October 1 Pete and I and several others boarded a train for London, where we were to catch another train that would take us to the reception center. Because our train was late getting into London, we missed the train to which we were to transfer and were pleased to be told we would spend the night in London. On our previous trips to London, hanging over our heads was the knowledge that we would have to return to our rather drab base. This time, Pete and I had a happy, carefree night in London celebrating our impending return to the U.S., our last fling in "Merry Olde England," although the England we had seen wasn't all that merry.

The next morning we caught the train to the reception center, where we remained for a week awaiting a States-bound ship. The very next day I got tagged for a day of K.P.—it always seemed to catch up with me. The problem was that almost everyone waiting there was either a staff or tech sergeant; thus, lots of stripes were seen working in the kitchen. Except for that one day, my time was my own, and with nothing to do, I sat in on both poker and crap games. I had about $150, most of which was winnings from recent 389th poker games, so I told myself that if I lost $50, that was it. I stuck $100 in a money belt that was to be reserved for use after I arrived home on the 23-day furlough that returnees were granted. By exercising both caution and common sense, I had run my $50 up to $250 by the end of the week, which did not include $50 that I loaned to an acquaintance who went broke. He was to mail the money to me as soon as he arrived home, but I never heard from him. Part of the $50 I had won from him, so perhaps he figured we were even.

Around the middle of October Pete and I finally boarded the *New Amsterdam*, a Dutch luxury liner converted to a troop carrier, for the eight-day trip to Boston, our port of debarkation. I would have preferred New York so that I could have the experience of seeing the Statue of Liberty appear on the horizon, but I was happy just to be heading for the U.S.A. Although the ship was crowded, conditions were fairly good. Pete and I were assigned to the same room, where we slept on double bunks similar to those used in England and were not too cramped for space, contrary to what I had heard was often the case. Our food was better than we had been accustomed to. We had been told that we would be less likely to get seasick if we did not skip meals and ate at least most of what was provided. Since I had never willingly skipped a meal, I had no intentions of starting now, so that advice was easy to follow. At any rate, I did not get seasick.

While poker games were available, crap games were the big thing. I stashed away all but $50 with which to try my luck. I decided that the best approach was to lay side bets on whoever had the dice; that is, I would place a bet with another person on whether or not the shooter would make his point. If I lost the bet, I would double the amount on the next bet; if I lost again, I would again double my bet, so that ultimately I would either lose enough consecutive bets to lose the $50 or come out ahead the amount of my first bet. If I won the first bet, I would use only my winnings for the next bet that I made. It may sound complicated but was actually quite simple, and it worked. By the end of three days I had run my winnings up to $450, at which point I decided that if I hit $500, I would quit. Before the end of the next day, I reached my goal, and that ended my gambling. I never got into another poker or dice game during the rest of my time in service. By today's standards, $500 is not much, but it was more than five months of my staff sergeant's base pay of $96.

The trip to Boston was not completely danger-free, for although the German sub threat was greatly diminished by late 1944, there was still the possibility of an attack. Because of the ship's speed, we were

271

not in a convoy. In peacetime the vessel was capable of making the trip in four days; but as a defense against subs, it changed direction every four minutes, following a zig-zag course that doubled the time to eight days. Two sub warnings were given, but both turned out to be drills rather than the real thing.

I thoroughly enjoyed the trip across the Atlantic, although if I had been on a regular troop ship under crowded conditions and typical army food, the trip would not have been so pleasant. We had a day or two of seas that were a little on the rough side but not bad. I even enjoyed standing by the rail and watching the bow of the ship cut through the waves and send spray flying. None of the days were cool enough to prevent our spending all the time we wished outside on the decks, and when we hit the Gulf Stream, it was like mild June days. The decks were full of men soaking up the sun; even the attendance at the crap games fell way off.

When the U.S. shoreline first appeared on the horizon, the rails were lined with homesick men. Several hours later I happily stepped onto American soil for the first time in nearly a year. Although I did not kneel and kiss the ground, I felt like it. We remained overnight at a base near Boston, from which I called Mary, with whom I had kept in touch since Shorty's death. I would have liked to visit her, but we were restricted to the base.

The next day Pete and I boarded separate trains, mine bound for Ft. Sheridan by Chicago, his for a California base. Although we corresponded until several years after the war, we never saw each other again. Though there was not that special bond that Shorty and I had shared, Pete and I were, nonetheless, close friends. We had been together since late June, 1943—sixteen months—and had shared a lot of experiences together. I was going to miss happy-go-lucky Pete and his big grin.

On October 28, 1944, after processing at Ft. Sheridan, I boarded the train to Quincy for a twenty-three-day furlough prior to reporting to the Santa Ana, California, Redistribution Center. This time I did not consider a surprise visit, for we had been warned against it during our processing. We were told that there had been cases of parents having heart attacks from the unexpected sight of a son at the front door; therefore, I called Mother and Dad from Fort Sheridan to let them know when I would arrive. They were waiting for me at the depot, and for the first time in almost a year and a half, I got behind the steering wheel of a car and drove home, where I had my first home-cooked meal since my June, 1943, furlough. Dad had a bottle of champagne on ice to celebrate my safe return. Mother and Dad, of course, had lots of questions about my year overseas; consequently, we stayed up until well past midnight going over events of the past year.

The next morning I called Jane to set a time to pick her up that evening, the first of many evenings we spent together during my leave, sometimes with her friends going with us. She and her mother (her father was dead), an excellent cook, had me over for dinner one evening. On November 4 we joined my parents and Mother's siblings and their spouses for an election night party. Fortunately, Jane was a Democrat, as was my family, so she was able to join in the glee as the election news on the radio reported Roosevelt running well ahead. I thought of how, when I had cast my absentee ballot, I had wondered about the chances of my being home by election day. Well, here I was!

Once again I enjoyed the luxury of sleeping in my own room and getting up when I felt like it. There were frequent family get-togethers and fishing trips (we had some beautiful November weather). Dad bought his gas at a service station run by one of Mother's cousins, who saw that I got all the gas I needed during my leave, so we were able to take a Sunday trip to St. Louis (the factory where Dad worked as a machinist operated the other six days). Except for our Sunday in St. Louis, I went with my parents to our small church, where I found myself the center of attention.

After a day or two at home, I was struck by the contrast between life in England and in the United States. True, some things were rationed—sugar, tires and gasoline, for example—but my parents and other family members seemed to get by quite well. Whereas in England most families, from my observations, used bicycles for short trips, I saw little of that in Quincy. Dad's gas allotment was sufficient to meet their needs, as was true of everyone I knew. People in the U.S. had no concept of the fear that accompanied air raids or what it was like to spend a night in a bomb shelter and then put in a full day at work. Blackouts were unknown except in coastal cities in the early months of the war, and even those had been lifted well before my return. In contrast with England's pubs, liquor of all kinds flowed freely in American taverns and night clubs. It was true that families with sons involved in combat lived with a continual fear of a telegram informing them that a son had become a battle casualty, and newspapers and the radio kept everyone informed of the battles being fought. However, from the standpoint of deprivation and hardship, it seemed to me that U.S. residents hardly were affected by the war. The Great Depression of the 30s was long gone, jobs were readily available, and wages were up. As John Blum expressed it, "It was a lovely war after all, with the fighting remote and prosperity returned."[15]

Another contrast that needs to be made is between combat as I experienced it and the Hollywood version in movies made during and after the war. Consider, for example, "Memphis Belle," centered around the first crew to complete its tour of missions with the 8th Air Force, although I have heard it was not the first. In that movie, the two waist gunners get into a fight while on a mission, the men chatter

---

[15] John Morton Blum, V Was for Victory (1976: Harcourt Brace Jovanovich), p. *116.*

constantly on the intercom, and the sound of exploding anti-aircraft fire and of the machine guns of attacking German fighters is quite audible. The real thing was quite different. If two crew members had fought while on a mission, they would have quickly become ex-members, or at least the one who initiated it would have. As for the use of the intercom, a disciplined crew used it only when necessary, such as when the pilot wanted to check on crew members, the bombardier announced "Bombs away," or a gunner informed the other men of the crew of the sighting of enemy planes. I am quite sure that if one of us had unnecessarily tied up the intercom while on a mission (no one ever did), Lt. Locke would have warned him. Because of the roar of four engines and the sound of the blast of wind coming through the waist windows and then past my turret, the only machine guns I could hear were those on our own plane. As noted earlier, flak explosions sometimes caused a sound like rain on a tin roof as the shock waves struck our fuselage, but I don't recall flak ever bursting close enough for me to hear the sound of the explosion. Also, if German fighters had come at us in the same way as portrayed in "The Memphis Belle," they would have been dead ducks. On our last mission, the Germans that attacked us from the front came quite close before breaking off, but not like in the movie.

The most realistic scene that I remember seeing in a war movie was in "Twenty Seconds over Tokyo," which I saw in mid-1945 while stationed at Lowry Field near Denver. The film is about the Doolittle-led raid on Tokyo in 1942. In one scene a B-25 ditches, and when it hit the water, it was so realistic that my upper body involuntarily jerked enough that my date looked over and asked, "Do you want to leave?" She knew about my ditching experience and understood my reaction. There was no need of our leaving, however. Surprisingly, I have never had a single dream about my combat experience, not that I remembered the next morning, at least.

The furlough flew by. I dreaded returning to the service routine and discipline, with part of my problem being that for the first time since entering service I would not be with anyone I knew and would have to make new friends. Like most servicemen, I had never liked and still did not like being a G.I. I didn't like the army kind of discipline, standing in line after line, sometimes being forced to obey orders for which I could see no purpose—in short, just having so little control over my circumstances. One factor that had made it tolerable from the time of my enlistment until now was close friends, especially the relationship I had enjoyed with the other members of my crew. Also, I had no inkling what kind of assignment I would get and did not like the uncertainty. I had the feeling that the best days of my time in service were behind me. As it turned out, I was right, for there were to be times when I wished I were back at Hethel serving as squadron gunnery sergeant.

When the day came for me to leave, Dad and Mother drove me to the depot, where we found a crowd waiting for the train I was to take. When the "All aboard" came, people began pushing and shoving to be the first on, and I found myself among the last to board the train. As a result, the first day and night of the trip to Santa Ana was a bad experience. I was unable to find a seat of any kind, and no civilian showed any inclination to give up his seat to a serviceman. Finally the conductor saw my plight and took me to a seat at the end of a car that was normally reserved for him. The seat had no reclining back, but it beat standing, and I appreciated the conductor's taking care of me.

The night seemed endless. I found sleeping without a reclining back to be impossible. The next day a conductor hinted that for a tip he might be able to find me a better seat, and a five-dollar tip produced a seat beside an attractive young lady who was going to California to visit her fiancé in the service. She was pleasant to talk to, and we went to the diner together. I have sometimes wondered what a ten-dollar tip might have brought.

On December 1 I reported to the redistribution center at Santa Ana, where I remained for five days awaiting permanent assignment. I quickly made friends with another ex-gunner. We visited Hollywood, where we went to the Hollywood Canteen, run by movie stars for servicemen. My main memory of the Canteen is of a pair of Mexican dancers. The young lady suddenly quit dancing and made a quick exit, then reappeared a few minutes later to continue the performance. A slip strap had broken. Another stop was Grauman's Chinese Theater, where movie premieres were held and where the hand and foot prints of Hollywood stars were placed in concrete in front of the theater. We also spent an evening listening to Tommy Dorsey's orchestra at a ballroom in a nearby seaside resort town. We hoped we might be able to pick up two girls there, but no luck. Nevertheless, as big band fans, we thoroughly enjoyed the Dorsey sound. A highlight of the evening came during the intermission when Dorsey's drummer—I am not positive, but think he was Buddy Rich—played a long drum solo. He was outstanding.

The food at the Santa Ana Redistribution Center was excellent. On a scale of 1-10, I'd have given it a 10. Not only was it well prepared, but also we had a choice of entrees—I didn't have to just take what was slapped on my tray. One meal even included lobster, which I had never eaten before. This mess hall was limited to the returnees from overseas. Of the several bases where I was stationed during my three years in service, this was the only place where I heard not one complaint about the food. Needless to say, we were not served spam or powdered eggs, two regulars in the 448th and 389th mess halls. It was the last special treatment I was to get as a combat veteran.

# CHAPTER 15: LOWRY FIELD

On December 6 came my orders to report to Lowry Field at Denver. I was pleased with the assignment, for my previous experience with the city while I was stationed at Buckley Field in 1943 had been a good one. On reporting at Lowry, I was assigned to an office as a clerk/typist. I liked the people I worked with; but in contrast with my duties while I was in the squadron bombardier's office after we ditched, I found the work here to be monotonous. Furthermore, we had so many personnel because of the large number of overseas returnees for whom assignments had to be found that we did not have enough work to keep everyone busy. It seemed to me that it would have made much more sense to have assigned me to one of the aerial gunnery schools, where I could have shared my ditching experience and given advice about ditching procedures to students, but that would have been too logical for the AAF, I guess. One of the main shortcomings of my pre-combat training had been in that area.

Shortly after my arrival at Lowry, I received a letter from Henrietta Reed, Kenneth Reed's mother, asking for information about the ditching. That was the beginning of an on-going correspondence for about the next ten years. She was the best letter writer of anyone with whom I have ever corresponded. Her letters sometimes made me smile, at other times touched me deeply, as did the following quotation, which exemplifies the way in which she faced her beloved Ken's death:

And as for Ken, I understand that both John Hortenstine and Errol Self tried to keep him up. This knowledge is of superlative comfort to us. It was just one of those things, Dale. And we are so grateful that seven of that splendid twelve are still here. We have looked the facts in the face from the beginning. I firmly believe that the five are all right. Why wouldn't they be, Dale? They were fine fellows, and they, with all of you that day, were doing their duty, a duty of great difficulty and a duty essential to the welfare of our fine country. Human beings are often unbelievably kind and good and brave. And so there is no doubt but what their Creator is even more so.

She and her husband, a professor at Cornell University, lived in Ithaca, New York, and she sometimes wrote descriptions of the area which brought them to life in my imagination. She was a remarkable woman. We corresponded until shortly before her death from cancer in the mid-1950s.

Arthur Delclisur's mother and Ralph Bryant's wife also wrote me requesting information. I did not, of course, tell Mrs. Bryant that her husband bore some responsibility for our having to ditch and had no desire to do so. I corresponded with Mrs. Delclisur for several years. She found it difficult to reconcile herself to Arthur's death, but since she was a widow, her having a problem is understandable.

A popular radio program was Ginny Simms' Purple Heart program. Ginny Simms, who began as a vocalist (one of my favorites) with Kay Kyser's orchestra and then made a few movies, sang and interviewed recipients of the Purple Heart on her show. About the middle of December, Mrs. Reed wrote me that our co-pilot, Lt. Self, was going to appear on the program, but her letter did not arrive until after his appearance. Mrs. Reed, however, sent me a copy of the script that she had obtained from the radio network, and when I read it, I was furious. The script had Lt. Self piloting the plane, whereas he had probably never once been behind the controls and was in the waist when we ditched. The Command Pilot, in this case Capt. Bryant, always sat in the co-pilot's seat, and Lt. Self was simply available if needed. No mention was made of Lt. Locke. In addition, the script contained several other departures from fact. For example, it read, "Limping back home over the North Sea, his plane was caught by Nazi fighters and shot down," but actually, all the attacks came while we were over the continent. Then, according to the script, not only was Self's back broken, but also his right shoulder and right leg, in spite of which (to quote the script) "he paddled around, using only one arm, since his legs were paralyzed and tried to save his fellow crewmen" (Superman had nothing on him!). Also, he, rather than John Hortenstine, tried to help Ken Reed, and only three rather than seven of the crew were saved. In view of Self's freeing Pete in spite of a broken back, the network had a good story; there was no need of all the fiction. I did not know, of course, if Self was responsible for twisting the facts; even if he wasn't, however, I felt it reprehensible for him to go along with it.

Since I was free to go off base whenever I was not working, I spent most of my evenings in Denver. On one of my trips to town soon after my arrival at Lowry Field, I ran into a girl, Bessie, whom my friend Steve had dated when we were stationed at Buckley Field in early 1943. We dated frequently for several weeks until our relationship came to an abrupt halt one evening. As we were sitting at a table in a nightclub, a lieutenant whom she knew came up to our table, talked for a few minutes and then left. Shortly afterwards, Bessie excused herself to go to the ladies' room. After waiting for about fifteen minutes, I realized what had happened: she had taken off with the lieutenant. The last half of the phrase "an officer and a gentleman" did not apply to him, and I decided Bessie was no lady. Not long after that unfortunate incident, I found solace in Helen, to whom I was introduced by a mutual friend. She was prettier than Bessie and more fun to be with, so I came out ahead after all. We frequently dated, but never got to the "going steady" point.

One evening when I picked up Helen at her apartment, I said, "I love fried oysters and oyster soup. Can you recommend a good restaurant for that?"

"Sure can," she answered. We called for a taxi and were seated in the restaurant a half-hour later. As we looked at the menu, Helen asked if I had ever tried raw oysters.

"No, and I don't plan to," I told her.

She insisted that anyone who likes oysters cooked should also like them raw, but I wasn't convinced. She wasn't ready to give up, though, and I finally agreed that we would split a half dozen on one condition: if I didn't like the first one, she would eat the rest. She promptly agreed.

That was my introduction to raw oysters. I knew I wasn't going to like them, but sprinkled with some pepper and dipped in the sauce that the waiter brought, I reluctantly had to admit that she was right. They were good. I ate my three, and she ate hers. That was the first of several times that we had raw oysters.

Apparently I got a little careless about the frequency with which I wrote Jane, my Quincy girlfriend, for a month or so after meeting Helen, I received a letter from Jane in which she lodged a strong complaint about my not writing often enough. Her letter caused me to think that she might be viewing our relationship somewhat differently than I. While I liked her and enjoyed being with her, I had never contemplated marriage, and I wondered if perhaps she was. Consequently, I decided I had better play it safe—I returned her photo together with a letter calling it quits. Although I didn't ask for it, I thought she would return a photo of myself that I had given her, but I heard nothing more from her. Not long after my discharge, I ran into her at a bar, and we spent an hour or two talking with nothing being said about the past. That was the last time I saw her.

I don't know why Mother did it, but when I was home on my November 1944 leave, she gave me a ring to wear which was a family heirloom. It was one which my great-grandfather had had made from the first nugget he found in 1849, when he was one of those involved in the California gold rush. Engraved on the crest was a tiny pick, pan, and shovel, the emblem of the forty-niners. One day when I glanced at my hand, my heart sank. The ring was gone. I dreaded telling Mother about its loss and wrote two or three letters without mentioning it. One evening about a week after I lost the ring, as I sat talking to the man who bunked next to me, an acquaintance whose bunk was nearby came over, held out his hand and said, "Do either of you have any idea what's on this ring? I found it in the grass outside our building."

I could hardly believe what I saw. It was my ring. I told him that I had lost it and explained its significance. He immediately gave it to me and refused to accept anything in the way of a reward. I thought about mailing the ring home, but because I was unwilling to chance its being lost in transit, I put it in a small box and placed it in the bottom of my foot locker. I had no intentions of wearing it again.

On April 12 while I was at the office where I worked, someone came in with the news of President Roosevelt's death. I, as well as the others in the office, was shocked. It hardly seemed possible that the man who had been president since I was eleven years old was gone. No one could fill his shoes, I thought. Over the following months of the war, however, I was pleasantly surprised at the way in which the former vice-president, Harry Truman, stepped in and handled his new responsibilities. I was one of those who, in 1948, was happily surprised at his defeat of Thomas Dewey and laughed at the Chicago *Tribune*'s premature headline about Dewey's winning the election.

On May 8 came the news that the war in Europe was over. I was eager to catch the bus into Denver, pick up Helen and join the celebration that I knew would be going on. Unfortunately, my plans were quickly shelved, for an order was issued that we were all restricted to the base. No reason was given. Possibly the rationale was that until Japan was defeated, we in the military had no business celebrating; or since the war in the Pacific was going so well, perhaps the big brass thought we could wait and do all our celebrating at once when Japan surrendered.

I continued working in the office to which I was first assigned until late May. Then I was told that the sergeant in charge wanted to see me. He was a buck sergeant (most of us as ex-combat men outranked him by one or two stripes) who had not been overseas. He had recently been brought in from another office to replace our previous sergeant, who had been transferred. He was a little stand-offish and was not nearly as well-liked. When I walked into the office that he shared with Lt. Wirtz, his superior officer, he said he was transferring me to Keesler Field in Mississippi, one of the least desirable posts in the Air Forces.

"Why?" I demanded.

"Because you're not keeping busy," he replied.

"You know as well as I that there are too many men assigned to this office. Have I ever given any indication of not being willing to do anything I was asked to do?" I was angry, and I am sure it showed. I had not, he said.

"Then why pick on me? If you felt I wasn't busy enough, why didn't you give me work to do? I can't manufacture it. Why didn't you give me some warning that you were unhappy with my performance?"

He remained silent, apparently trying to decide how to respond. I stood there for a moment, waiting for him to speak up. Being under the control of someone whom I outranked and who had not been overseas irritated and frustrated me. The fact that he had not been overseas should have had no effect on my attitude, but because I was angry, it did. Also, it was the first time my job performance had ever been criticized, and it hurt. Finally I said, "If you're determined to transfer me, at least see that it is a better place than Keesler."

At that point Lt. Wirtz, who had seemed to be busy reading some papers in front of him, spoke up. "I'll arrange a transfer to a line office here at Lowry." I was gratified that he spoke kindly and smiled. He apparently felt I had at least some justification for being angry but figured it best not to leave the sergeant and me in the same office. "Go see the sergeant at the front desk in the next office."

"Thank you, sir," I said. He had been the head of the office ever since I had been assigned to it, and I had always had a good relationship with him. I saluted him and left the office. As I walked out, he was making a phone call.

My new job was in a line office located on the ramp where B-29s were parked. As the only typist, I kept busy most of the time, enjoyed being around planes again, and liked the other men in the office, who soon became friends. As long as I completed the work which he gave me, the lieutenant in charge of the office seemed to have no problem with my gabbing with the others. As the only one in the office who had been in combat, I found myself frequently answering questions about my experiences. One of the men said, "How about writing an account of your ditching?" I went to my typewriter and turned one out before the day was over, which the other men took turns reading. I didn't expect it to make quite the impression on them that it did.

A few days after transferring to the line office, I requested and received permission to go through a B-29 that was parked in front of our office. Compared to the B-24 and the B-17, the B-29's longer length and wingspan were obvious from the outside, but when I climbed into the cockpit area and looked down the tunnel that one had to crawl through to get to the waist and tail section, I was even more impressed by its size. I envied the B-29 crew their more sophisticated equipment. For example, since the guns could be remotely controlled, the waist windows were kept closed, thus eliminating the blast of cold air that we experienced in the waist and tail of the B-24. Moreover, luxury of luxuries, the entire plane was pressurized and heated, doing away with the wearing of oxygen masks and the fear of frostbite.

One evening in late June Jack Benny entertained the Lowry personnel. With him were his wife, Mary Livingston, Rochester, and Jerry Colonna, all members of Benny's radio program cast. An outdoor stage was erected so that everyone who wished to watch could do so. I was quite a ways back from the stage, but could see the entertainers well enough. I expect Benny had his own sound system, for I had no problem hearing what was said. I didn't think it likely that Lowry had one that good.

One of the men, whose name I have forgotten, who came into the line office was a master sergeant who had been in the Pacific theater. After discovering that we both were from Quincy, we struck up a friendship. He was assigned to the same barracks as I; however, rather than being in a large room with 75-100 other men, as I was, he had the luxury of being in an adjoining private room with only three other men. Not long after we met, one of the men in his room was transferred, and I was invited to move into his room. For the first time since my enlistment, I had some privacy. The room also offered two other advantages: we didn't have to turn our lights out at a set time, which I think was 10:30, and we were not subject to bed check, so that if we went into Denver, we did not have to be back at any particular time.

Not long after my transfer, I was surprised to run into Gene, the sergeant who had taken Buck and me into San Antonio during our week of restriction to base preceding the start of basic training. He was no longer a sergeant, however. He had got into an argument with a superior non-com at Kelly Field and struck him, with the result that he lost his stripes and was transferred. He was at Lowry to attend a school of some kind. He and I spent a few evenings together in Denver before he finished school and was transferred.

In June I received a ten-day furlough. After checking train and plane schedules, I found that I could get to Quincy about as quickly and at a fraction of the cost by taking the train from Denver as I could by flying to St. Louis and then taking the train to Quincy. Mother and Dad met me at the depot, and I once again enjoyed getting behind the steering wheel and driving home, this time to a different address. As Mother had already written me, they had sold the big, two-story home where we were living when I enlisted and bought a smaller one-level house with basement that involved less upkeep.

Once again I enjoyed family get-togethers, fishing trips with my grandfather (Dad was unable to get time off during the week), and the luxury of sleeping in my own room. Since I had split with Jane, I called a girl whom I had frequently dated prior to enlisting to see if she might be available. She was, and we went out three or four evenings. As in my previous leaves, the day of my return to duty came all too soon. This time, though, saying goodbye was made easier by the hope that the war would not last too much longer and that I would be back home sooner rather than later.

Another friend who showed up unexpectedly in late July was Buck, with whom I had enlisted in the Air Forces and parted from on finishing armorers school. He was still a private first class, the rank we had received on finishing the school, and was at Lowry to attend another school prior to being shipped overseas. Our friendship came to an abrupt halt, though, when I went into Denver one evening and found him with Helen, to whom I had introduced him. I had originally intended to remain on base that evening, which he knew, then changed my mind. Although Helen and I dated frequently, we were not tied to each other and we both dated others, but I felt that his underhanded approach was in very poor taste. Buck left us, and I never saw him again. Helen defended herself on the grounds that she could date anyone she wanted to, which I readily admitted. I was primarily irked at Buck. Helen and I continued to go out together, though not as often as before.

The news that an atomic bomb had been dropped on Hiroshima on August 6 brought joy to the inhabitants of Lowry Field. Surely the Japanese would face up to their inevitable defeat now and surrender. We kept the radio on at the office to get the latest news.

The evening after the dropping of the atomic bomb, as Helen and I came out of a restaurant, an M.P. stopped me.

"Where's your cap?" he asked.

My cap was in my hand. Having just exited the restaurant, I was getting ready to put it on, as I stated to him.

"Doesn't matter. You were outside without your cap on." Technically he was right, but I had never heard of anyone, even a buck private M.P. who had never been out of the States, such as this one, interpreting regulations quite that literally. It seemed that men who had spent their entire service career States-side were determined to give me a hard time. I was not looking for special treatment because I had been overseas nor looking down on those who had not—one of my best friends had not—but I did resent being singled out this way by someone who had had the good fortune to spend all his time in the U.S.

Though difficult, I held my temper and tried to reason with him, and then Helen tried to reason with him, but to no avail. He took my pass, which meant that I had to return to the base. As a result, I was restricted to camp for one week, and it was during that week that V.J.

(Victory over Japan) day occurred. Everyone was in town celebrating the end of the war, and there I was, stuck in camp by an M.P. who, as far as I was concerned at that point, deserved the firing squad. I even went to my C.O. to plead for my pass, but he said his hands were tied, which was not really true. My permanent pass was on his desk; all he had to do was hand it to me. At that moment I had never disliked anyone in my twenty-four years as much as I did that M.P. and my C.O., not even the Germans who had shot at me. What a contrast, I thought, between this C.O. and Major Sisson, my 389th C.O., who undoubtedly would have sent me into town without hesitation; in fact, he would probably not have given the week's restriction to begin with. The only consolation 1 had was that a friend had spent his last cent and felt it wasn't worth going into town if he couldn't even buy a drink, so we spent the day commiserating with each other. My attitude wasn't helped when I heard some of the men talking later about what a great time they had.

A point system based on length of service, time overseas, and awards was being used to determine the order in which men were discharged. Each award (medals, oak leaf clusters, and battle stars) was worth five points. Each month in service added one point; each month overseas, one point. The minimum total to qualify for discharge was initially set at eighty-five. Much to my dismay, I had only eighty. Had I been able to finish my missions, I would have had at least eighty-five; thus, I was penalized for being injured and taken off flying status. My morale hit a new low. I went to our headquarters and asked a clerk to check to see if another battle star in addition to the two that I knew of had been authorized for the 448th and 389th. Since each one was worth five points, I needed only one for immediate discharge. After a few minutes he returned to say that none had. Feeling very sorry for myself, I returned to my barracks.

In September the minimum was lowered; I was at last eligible for discharge. I learned that anyone who could show proof of a job offer from a Denver employer could be processed at Lowry Field and thus speed up his discharge; otherwise, one would have to go through the red tape of waiting for the processing of orders transferring him to a discharge center in his native state. I decided to try to do what many Lowry men were doing: come up with a job offer from someone with the understanding that it would not be followed up on. I went to the owner of a night club which I frequently visited with friends, explained the situation to him, and received a letter from him that he would hire me upon my discharge. I was so anxious to get out of uniform that being guilty of a deception did not weigh at all heavily on my conscience.

A few days later on October 4, exactly two years, eleven months and one day after enlisting, I received my discharge. One of my pet peeves about the Air Forces had been all the lines in which we had to wait, but waiting in line several times during the discharge process did not bother me one bit. At the last table we stopped by at the Lowry Field separation center was a recruiting officer. His suggestion that I enlist in the Air Forces reserves in order to preserve my staff sergeant rank met with my very quick and emphatic "NO WAY!" I put all the feeling I could into both words. At last I was free and headed for home via one last train ride in uniform. There were civvies in my immediate future, and I could hardly wait. I celebrated my discharge that evening with Helen and a few friends, then took the train for Quincy the next morning.

Once again Mother and Dad were waiting to pick me up when my train pulled in. What a joy I felt to see them and know that I was home for good. Because of the weight I had gained during my three years in the AAF, most of the clothes I had owned before enlisting did not fit too well. The next morning, therefore, I put on my uniform one more time, and Mother and I went shopping for new clothes. I was perfectly capable of picking out my own, of course, but Mother was not about to miss the fun of helping.

Had I examined my discharge papers more closely before I left Denver, I might have gone back to the headquarters building and confronted—and perhaps assaulted—a certain clerk. When I looked over my discharge after arriving home, I found that I had been credited with *two* additional battle stars that were authorized during the time I was with the 389th; thus, instead of eighty points, I had ninety. The clerk had probably not bothered to check the records when I made my inquiry at headquarters. I should have been discharged weeks before I was.

**At his mothers request, the body of Lt. Arthur Delclisur was returned to the United States in 1948 and a military funeral was held. Mrs. Delclisur sent photos of the funeral to the author**

A few years ago a friend and I were reminiscing about our WWII

years. He summed it up well when he said, "I wouldn't take a million dollars for the experience, and I wouldn't take a million dollars to go

through it again!"

# CHAPTER 16: A CIVILIAN AGAIN

Making the transition from being a G.I. to being a civilian posed no problem at all for me.  It was as if I had never been gone except that none of my friends had been discharged yet.  Since the weather was nice all through October, Dad and I resumed our Saturday fishing trips, and during the week my grandfather and I went occasionally to the private lake which he had permission to fish.  It was a joy, too, once again to be a part of the frequent family get-togethers with my grandparents and Mother's siblings and their spouses.

One of the benefits available to veterans was up to a year of unemployment compensation.  I no longer remember what the monthly amount was, but it was quite adequate to meet my needs, especially since I was living with my parents, who refused to accept anything from me.  Dad was making good money as a machinist, their home was paid for, and they felt that it cost very little more to feed three than two.  I did not have to be in a hurry, therefore, to reach a decision on a job.  I gave some thought to going back to my machinist's trade and was offered a job at Dad's factory, but because machine shops are frequently very noisy, I feared that working in one could be hard on my one good ear. Furthermore, I did not relish the prospect of spending the rest of my working years turning out parts on a machine. It could get very boring.

After a few months of hunting for a job without finding one that I was willing to take, I decided I had better take advantage of the G.I. Bill, which would pay all my expenses if I went to college, plus a monthly allotment for living expenses. I enrolled at Quincy College (now Quincy University) in September 1946, with the idea of becoming a history teacher. I had enjoyed reading history ever since I was in grade school; also, I felt that my World War II service provided a good background for a high school history teacher. Though not well known, Quincy College offered me a good curriculum and small classes and, perhaps most important, would let me live at home. After being away for three years, I wasn't ready to leave family and friends quite yet.

In the seven years which had elapsed since graduating from high school, I had forgotten all the grammar I ever knew; however, I was one of those people who write reasonably well in spite of not knowing grammar. At any rate, I did well enough in the first semester of my freshman composition class that my instructor recommended that I be permitted to forgo the second semester of composition and be enrolled in creative writing. He also believed that I was cut out to be an English teacher and encouraged me to switch from a history to an English major, which I did. In later years when I found myself spending hours grading themes, many of which were poorly written, I sometimes wondered if I had made a mistake; however, as things developed, I think I made the right decision.

Because I was twenty-five when I enrolled at Q.C., I wanted to get my diploma as quickly as possible. As a result of maintaining a high grade-point average, after the first semester I was permitted to take a heavier-than-normal course load; thus, by taking extra courses and going to summer school, I completed the four years of undergrad work in June 1949, two years and nine months after I began. I subsequently received an M.A. degree from Drake University and later qualified for a media specialist certificate by completing twenty-four semester hours at Southern Illinois University at Edwardsville, Illinois.

My three close friends, Carl Eyre, Ken Plowman and Bob Dinkheller were discharged a few weeks after I arrived home, and we once again resumed our nights out together, which invariably consisted of making the rounds of the night clubs and taverns. I'm sure my parents were quite unhappy with my drinking, but they said nothing. Fortunately, I went with them to church each Sunday, and after a while my conscience began to work on me. I liked my friends, however, and didn't want to break with them. In June 1946, help came from an unexpected quarter.

Bob had begun going steady with the girl who later became his wife, and I frequently double-dated with him and Marcia. Marcia decided that she knew someone who was a better match for me than the girl I was dating and, after receiving my permission, arranged a blind date for me with a church friend. That date led to another and another. Then about two weeks after we had met, when I walked the young lady—and that is exactly what she was, a lady—to her door at the end of our evening and asked about seeing her the next evening, she said, "I'm sorry, but I can't go out with you any more."

"Why not?" I asked.

"Because I don't want to go with anyone who drinks."

I knew she was a Baptist, but I didn't know until then how strong her convictions were. I had never run into a girl like that before. I explained how my conscience had been troubling me and that I was ready to quit the drinking. Much to my relief, she agreed to give me another chance. From then on we began dating more and more frequently until we were spending six evenings together each week. Insisting that she needed one night to do her laundry and recuperate, she drew the line there. On April 9, 1949, a few weeks before I was to receive my degree from Quincy College, Mary Elizabeth Stickler became Mary Elizabeth VanBlair.

In spite of all the dating on top of a heavy class load, I managed to graduate with honors. One mitigating factor was that I always came up with a class schedule that had no more than one class on Tuesday and Thursday, days which I set aside for studying and preparing assignments.

After my graduation from Q.C., Mary E. (that was how her grandmother addressed her, and I preferred using three rather than six syllables for what I hoped would be a long married life) and I moved to Vandalia, Illinois, where I had been hired to teach high school English for $2700 (that was for a year, not a month). We quickly became close friends of two of my fellow teachers and their wives, who couldn't understand how we could tithe to our church and still get by on our salary better than they did. We knew why, however: God made it possible.

Mary E. and I both wanted children; but when a hysterectomy in 1952 ended our hopes of her conceiving, we decided to look into adopting and began exploring various possibilities. Nothing, however, fell into place.

Although we were happy in Vandalia, in 1953 we agreed that I ought to seek a position with a better-paying school system. In early summer I received notice of an opening at Champaign (Illinois) Junior High School that sounded interesting, but when I got around to responding, I saw that I had overlooked a deadline for applying that had already passed. So much for that, I thought. A few days later, however, I received a phone call from the principal, who asked me to come for an interview. I went, was interviewed and was hired on the spot.

A few weeks after getting settled in Champaign, we learned that the Illinois Children's Home and Aid had an office in nearby Urbana and filed an adoption application. During the next several months we went through numerous interviews and home visits, then were told that we had been approved and would be getting a child. In late May 1954, we received a beautiful three-month-old baby girl whom we named Deborah Kay. Now we were certain that God was behind the circumstances that led us to Champaign.

The next school year I was assigned to a new junior high school, where I served as department chairman. Thinking we were settled permanently, we contracted in early 1956 to have a house built. In the spring I received notice of an opening in the English Department of the high school in Belleville, Illinois, which I tossed in the wastebasket and then, on impulse, retrieved. In spite of being satisfied in Champaign and having the house under construction, getting back into high school teaching appealed to me. With my wife's approval, I applied and was hired. I saw a bit of irony in my pending return to Belleville, which I had visited during the week I spent at Scott Field after enlisting.

*Dale VanBlair*

Our house under construction was in a new subdivision. When we talked to our builder about our situation, he said, "I've raised my prices $1000 since you signed your contract. Lots of people are driving through the subdivision and looking. If you will put a for sale sign in front of your house, the fact that it's only a few weeks from completion is bound to sell it. Add $1000 to your contract price." Not all builders would have been as cooperative. We followed his advice, and before it was finished, we sold the house ourselves for a profit of $1000, which wasn't a bad return on the small amount of earnest money we had put down.

As soon as the school year ended, Mary E. and I left Debbi with our next-door neighbors and drove to Belleville to look for a house. After looking at several with two different realtors, we were discouraged. We found something wrong with most of the houses, and the two or three that we liked were priced above what we thought we could afford. As we drove back to our motel late that afternoon, we passed an attractive home with a "For sale by owner" sign in the front yard.

"Stop," said Mary E. "Let's look at it."

"It's sure to be more than we can afford," I replied. "It's a waste of time."

She insisted on investigating. "We've nothing to lose. I'll go to the door and find out what they're asking."

I waited while she went to the front door, rang the doorbell and then talked for a few minutes to the lady who came to the door. She came back smiling.

"The price is almost exactly the same as the one we were having built in Champaign. We can look at it right now."

We went through the house, liked it very much and signed a contract the next day.

Two years after we moved to Belleville, when Debbi developed a skin rash, Mary E. called the pediatrician. "Could it be inherited?" he asked.

"No," replied Mary E. "She's adopted."

"Oh, I knew that," the doctor said, then quickly added, "Say, how would you like to adopt another one?"

He went on to explain that he was taking care of a Canadian citizen whose American husband had deserted her. Because she already had a child, she felt that she couldn't adequately handle the financial burden of another one. We agreed to pay all expenses connected with the birth of her baby, and a few days after the mother gave birth on December 6, 1958, we took home another beautiful baby girl, whom we named Karen Beth. We believed that God had been behind my retrieving the notice of the Belleville opening from the wastebasket, our finding the house in Belleville, and the circumstances which led to our adopting Karen.

In Belleville I taught English in the high school and rhetoric and American literature in the junior college, both of which belonged to District 201. After a few years, all but one of my classes were on the junior college level. In 1965, after the voters approved forming a separate junior college district, I had to decide whether to stay with the high school or go with the junior college. Because our department chairman was going with the junior college, my principal asked me to stay with the high school to become chairman of the English Department. That put me in a quandary. I liked my junior college schedule, which now consisted of all American literature classes, but at the same time I felt attracted to the position of English Department chairman. I liked our principal and knew I could work with him. Also, as chairman I would have an opportunity to work with curriculum and, hopefully, effect some improvement. Because of the department's size, I would teach only one class and thus have time to visit classes to see what was going on and to develop some ideas I had for the department. After several changes of mind, I finally decided to stay with the high school, where I supervised from thirty to forty English teachers each year until my retirement in 1982. During my tenure, we made some changes in the curriculum that worked out quite well, and I was fortunate in being able to hire some teachers fresh out of college who developed into outstanding educators. Book salesmen who called on me told me that we had one of the best English Departments in Illinois.

When the 1981-82 school year started I had not given much thought to retirement. However, in a few weeks I began to seriously consider it. The school district was having money problems, and one step it took to cut back on expenses was to encourage teachers at the top of the salary schedule, such as I, to retire so that they could be replaced by teachers with little or no experience who could be hired at greatly reduced salaries.

I decided to take advantage of the incentives being offered to encourage older teachers to retire and in June 1982 ended my career as an educator.

In 1986 we went with three other couples who were close friends on a three-week tour of Ireland, Scotland and England, in that order. I was especially anxious to visit London, where our tour ended and where I had spent several weekends and my convalescent furlough during the war. I found that about the only changes that had taken place were the many new buildings that had been erected in the bombed-out areas. All of the devastated area around St. Paul's Cathedral was now built up. However, the hotels I had stayed in were still there, Piccadilly Circus and Trafalgar Square were as I remembered them, and double-deck buses like I had ridden were still providing transportation. Moreover, when we used the underground for transportation during our free time, I had no problem, for it also seemed unchanged.

Mary E. and I took three extra days at the end of the tour to visit the Norwich area, where I had been based during the war. I had arranged with Pat Everson of Seething, the village adjacent to the 448th base, to meet us at the train station and give us a tour of the area. As a child, Pat had watched our B-24s as they took off for and returned from missions. She retained a keen interest in the 448th and, a few years later, began collecting materials pertaining to the group. She ultimately assembled a mass of 448th data and gives freely of her time to respond to requests for information from the group's veterans, members of their families, and others. Pat and her husband, Ron, took a leading role in restoring the 448th control tower and turning it into a museum honoring the group. When she took us to the tower, I went to a window that overlooked a section of the one remaining original runway. I thought of Shorty and the other members of my crew and wondered how many, if any, of those who survived the ditching were still alive. It hardly seemed possible that over forty-two years had elapsed since we had taken off from this field to drop bombs on German targets.

**American flag and plaques honoring the men of the 448th displayed on a wall of the church in Seething, England.**

**Memorial to the 448th in the cemetery adjacent to the Seething church.**

From the control tower, Pat took us took us to the nearby village of Seething. Though lacking the grandeur of the cathedrals which we had seen on our tour, the small thatch-roofed church with stone walls fascinated me. One end of the church incorporates a tower dating back to early Norman times. Floor levels in the church date from the fourteenth century. It has a 1485 font and three bells manufactured in 1634, 1638 and 1721. On one wall is a painting that is centuries old, but I do not have its date recorded. As much as I appreciated its antiquity, I saw something on another wall that meant even more to me: a large American flag, beneath which was a memorial to the men of the 448th. How I appreciated their remembering us!

In late August 2002, Mary E. was diagnosed with a very active bladder cancer and was given three options. (1) Since the cancer had not spread, the bladder could be removed. At her age of 83 the operation would be risky, but if successful, she would be cancer-free. (2) The doctor could remove as much of the cancer as possible and then repeat the operation when necessary. The operation would involve much less risk, but within three or four years the cancer would get beyond control. (3) Chemotherapy could be used to slow down the cancer's growth, but within about four years it would be fatal. I had watched my mother, an aunt and an uncle die from cancer and didn't want to see Mary E. go through that; hence, I told her I preferred the first option in spite of the risk, and she agreed.

The operation was performed in early September and went well. For four days her condition improved, and I was elated. Then the bottom dropped out. She developed a urinary infection which the doctors could not control with antibiotics. Had she been younger, the surgeon said, he would have done exploratory surgery and perhaps have been able to take care of the problem, but she could not possibly survive a second operation. She went into a coma and died September 10, 2002.

As I stood by her bed and watched the pulse at the base of her neck beat more and more slowly and then cease, the tears coursed down my cheeks, but not for her. I knew that because of her faith, my beloved wife was now in the presence of God. No more sickness, no more pain, no more tears. In spite of how much I knew I would miss her, I was happy for her. Even if God had suddenly said, "Would you like to have her back?" I'd have replied, "No, thank you. But you might take me!"

Mary E and I always tried to put God first in our lives and relied on Him to help us make decisions, such as the moves we made. He brought Mary E. through several serious illnesses, two of which could very well have been fatal. I am convinced that He enabled me to hold my breath as long as I did before surfacing when we ditched and that I would not have survived my time in that very cold water without His intervention. I also credit Him with bringing me through spinal meningitis in spite of the flight surgeon's prediction to my C.O. that I would not be back.

# EPILOGUE

Shorty's fiancée, Mary, and I have kept in touch throughout the years. In the early 1950s she married Bill DeAvilla, who had been a close friend of Shorty prior to the war. On their honeymoon they came through Vandalia, where I was teaching, and stopped to visit. Mary's sister married one of Shorty's brothers; thus, Mary has remained very close to the Spadaforas. I have visited them and Shorty's family in Boston several times. Incidentally, they never called him Shorty; that was strictly his Air Forces nickname. To them, he was Albert. When I first met him, the nickname had already been attached to him, and I think it was a few weeks before I knew his given name. He never gave any evidence of objecting to it and sometimes even referred to himself as Shorty.

I corresponded with Al Locke and Pete Paez for several years after the war before losing touch with both. Al took engineering at the University of Oklahoma. Pete went to work in California, but I no longer remember what he was doing.

In the 1970s I found out about and joined the 2$^{nd}$ Air Division Association, which was formed after the war for veterans who had flown on B-24s in England (all B-24 groups were assigned to the 2$^{nd}$ Air Division). From that organization's membership roster, I obtained John Hortenstine's address in Abingdon, Virginia, in 1986, and we began corresponding. John became a chemical engineer after the war, was recalled to duty during the Korean War, as noted in Chapter 13, then returned to chemical engineering. When the 448$^{th}$ held a reunion in Hampton, Virginia, in 1992, we met there and had a great time reminiscing. When we talked about Self, our co-pilot, John said that he rarely went off base with other officers, including those of our crew. He was primarily interested in one thing: women. "If it wore high heels," said John, "Self was after it." He had a good relationship with our other officers; he simply wanted no interference or distraction when he went to town. John did not marry until 1971 and had one son who, at the time that we met, was in high school. John died suddenly of a heart attack on November 9, 1992.

For several months in 1986 I attempted to locate Al Locke before learning through the University of Oklahoma Alumni Association that he had died. Then, in August 2000, his granddaughter, Melinda Staley of Colorado Springs, sent an email to the B-24 web site on the Internet to see if she could find anyone who might have information about her grandfather. Fortunately, I read her email, and we have established a close relationship through visits in each other's homes and frequent contact via our computers. In 2002 Al Locke's daughter Linda and husband Richard (Melinda's parents) came with Melinda and her family to visit me. I am pleased that Melinda refers to me as her adopted grandfather.

Pat, Al's wife, remarried after his death in 1972 and lives in the state of Washington, as do Linda and Richard. In an email to Melinda in which she was responding to questions Melinda had asked about her grandfather, Pat mentioned that Jimmy Stewart was supposed to fly with us on our ditching mission but was taken off it. At that time Stewart was with the 2nd Air Division Headquarters, which were on our base. Since Al did not tell us about that when we were talking before the mission, I suspect that he found out about it later in talking to Stewart at the 389th officers' club. He had met Stewart when our group and Stewart's were at Sioux City at the same time. Had Stewart gone with us he might not have lived to make all those movies after the war.

Melinda and I have cooperated in trying to turn up additional information about such things as the planes we flew and the English boat that picked up our crew's survivors after the ditching. We learned that it was RML (Rescue Motor Launch) 498, which was in the 60th RML Flotilla based at Great Yarmouth. Her skipper was Lt. Doug Harding. Thanks to Alan Rowe, who served in the British Air-Sea Rescue Service and wrote an excellent book about it, I was put in touch with Les Coulson, one of RML 498's crew and was able to write and thank him for the role he played in saving my life. I hoped he might have a photo of 498 or of its crew, but he did not. Melinda and I have also set up a web site about the Alfred H. Locke crew, the address of which is www.geocities.com/b24gunr2000/index.html.

From time to time in recent years I have used my computer and other sources to try to track down the other members of my crew who might still be alive. In 1998 I located the family of Frank Cappello (Cappy), our radio operator, only to learn that he had died not long before. Then, in December 2001, as I was working on revising this narrative, I received an email from Roslyn Turochy, the niece of Arthur Delclisur, our bombardier who lost his life in our ditching. In doing genealogical research, she had fed the name Delclisur into a search engine on her computer, which had led her to the web site about our crew, from which she obtained my screen name. I was surprised to learn from Roslyn that, according to what she had been told, Arthur had a girl friend whom he was planning to marry when he returned home. In the conversations we had, he never mentioned a girl friend. As for Virgil Carroll, Pete Paez, Hank Boisclair, and Errol Self, I have been unable to turn up anything, thus suspect that I am the sole survivor of our crew.

# BIBLIOGRAPHY

Bailey, Mike. *Liberator Album.* Leicester, England: Midland Publishing Limited, 1998.

Blum, John Morton. *V Was for Victory.* New York: Harcourt Brace Jovanovich, 1976

Bowden, Ray. *Tales to Noses Over Berlin: The 8th Air Force Missions.* London: Design Oracle Partnership, 1996.

Hoseason, James. *The 1,000 Day Battle.* Lowestoft, England: Gillingham Publications, 1979.

McBride, Charles C. *Mission Failure and Survival.* Manhattan, Kansas: Sunflower University Press, 1989.

McManus, John C. *Deadly Sky: The American Combat Airman in World War II.* Novato, California: Presidio Press, Inc., 2000.

# ABOUT THE AUTHOR

Born in Quincy, Illinois, in 1921, DaleVanBlair enlisted in the Army Air Force in November 1942 and served as a tail gunner with a B-24 crew. On his eighteenth mission his crew led a formation of B-24s to Berlin and sustained fighter and flak damage that forced them to ditch in the frigid North Sea with the loss of five men. Van Blair's injuries resulted in his being grounded. Following his discharge in October 1945, he graduated from Quincy University and then taught high school English. For seventeen years prior to his retirement in 1982, he served as English Department chain man in a large high school in Belleville, Illinois, the city in which he still lives.

CPSIA information can be obtained
at www.ICGtesting.com
Printed in the USA
BVHW030046130519
548104BV00001B/1/P